COURAGE TO CARE, STRENGTH TO SERVE

Reflections on Community Service

by
Howard Zeiderman

Published by
TOUCHSTONES®
DISCUSSION PROJECT

About the Touchstones® Discussion Project
The Touchstones Discussion Project is a nonprofit organization founded on the belief that all people can benefit from the listening, speaking, thinking, and interpersonal skills gained by engaging in active, focused discussions. Since 1984, Touchstones has helped millions of students and others develop and improve these skills in school, work, and life. For more information about the Touchstones Discussion Project, visit www.touchstones.org.

©2009, 2013
by Touchstones Discussion Project
PO Box 2329
Annapolis, Maryland 21404
800-456-6542
www.touchstones.org

ISBN: 978-1-937742-30-0

Acknowledgments

We would like to thank the following for their help in the publication of this volume:

Harper and Row Publishers, Inc., for permission to reprint selections from *Letter from Birmingham Jail* and *Why We Can't Wait.* © 1963, 1964, by Martin Luther King, Jr.

Random House Inc., and Ralph Ellison for permission to reprint pp. 3-4 from *Invisible Man.*

Grove Press Inc., for permission to reprint pp. 36-38 from *The Autobiography of Malcolm X.* © 1965, by Alex Haley and Betty Shabazz.

Vernon Jordan, Jr., for permission to reprint his address "We Cannot Live for Ourselves Alone."

Table of Contents

Unit VI. Reflections on Peer Counseling

Unit VII. Reflections on Serving the Aging

TOUCHSTONES® DISCUSSION PROJECT

Using This Volume

The texts included in this collection can serve as valuable cornerstones in a course on community service. They illustrate what thoughtful people through history have had to say about issues with which humanity continues to wrestle. Such writings are valuable because they encourage reflection about the relationship of the self to the other. Dialogue that starts with sharing these texts can lead to new directions for further inquiry and action. In addition, thoughtful discussion about the importance of community service reinforces the development of learning skills and behaviors fundamental to the Touchstones Discussion Project method:

- Listening actively,
- Collaborating with people of different backgrounds,
- Thinking responsibly in situations of uncertainty,
- Teaching oneself, and
- Explaining one's ideas.

Purpose of Discussion

Touchstones discussion classes encourage all participants involved to engage actively in their own and one another's learning and to take responsibility for their own opinions. Participants should not try to compete to show how much they know or have memorized. Instead, honesty, exploration, and openness are key traits of successful participants in Touchstones discussions. When we listen to other perspectives, each of us helps the others to learn. A class that works together like this will become a group with a common purpose. An entire educational community that participates in classes like this—the school, teachers and students alike—will become an enlivened and enriched environment where everyone is valued and where inquiry into important questions happens naturally and productively.

In such a community, the highest value is placed on the courage to question our own beliefs. In questioning our own beliefs, we rely on collaboration from the entire group. This is so that we can each speak our opinions and ideas so all can hear, listen openly and respectfully, consider and analyze, and reflect on dilemmas, questions, and problems that do not have complete and simple solutions.

Choice of Texts

The texts in Touchstones are ideal for discussions that aim at cooperation among us all and that move us to look at opinions we take for granted. We may or may not change our viewpoints, but whatever we do, we will know better why we believe what we do. Just as importantly, we will have learned to work with others and to listen carefully to them. The skills and attitudes that result make a difference everywhere—in our classes, personal relationships, family interactions, and with our community.

The texts in Touchstones are short, so that they can be read easily during the beginning of class. No advance preparation is needed, although it may be helpful. Reading a text carefully at home in advance will likely mean a deeper engagement during the discussion, but this is not always possible.

Role of the Leader

The discussion on a Touchstones text is based on the tension between the text and our own perspective. The leader's role is two-fold: to keep the tension from moving us too far away from the text on the one hand, and from ensuring that our life experiences don't overrun the dialogue on the other. When the text becomes a launch pad to some abstract issue (such as, "Is there free will?" or "Is the individual more important than society?"), the discussion will lose focus. In those cases, the leader should bring us back to the central issue or issues in the text. On the other hand, if the discussion lingers too long on a small detail in the text, the leader can redirect the discussion to larger issues by asking why this detail is important and to provide examples from our own lives. This is not to say that the simple exchanging of stories or experiences with one another is fruitful. Rather, part of the discussion leader's role is to ask the participants to relate the story or experience to the text.

The leader does not direct the discussion. The leader's task is to create and preserve the conditions for a discussion and to make sure everyone is responsible to the text and to one another.

As class comes to a close, the leader will not wind-up or summarize the discussion. Instead, everyone is encouraged to have an opinion about what has been said in the discussion and how ideas may have shifted or been reinforced. Any summary will fall short of capturing the implications of the discussion for all of the participants and the work done by the group. In addition, when the conversation is ended without a summary, the conversation is more likely to continue on into the corridors and even at home.

Finally, neither the discussion leader (whether it's the teacher or a student) should be afraid of long silences or pauses in the dialogue. Let them happen. These "pregnant" pauses are often times when deep reflection occurs, making the discussion that follows even richer. These short stops in the discussion also create room for quieter students to enter the conversation. Everyone in the group should be mindful and attentive to those students who need these openings to feel comfortable speaking.

Opening Questions

After the selected text has been read aloud by someone in the group, the Touchstones discussion begins with a question asked by the teacher, or leader. (When possible, students may serve as the discussion leader.) It is helpful when all students write down a relevant question for the group to consider for discussion. Sharing these questions with the group often serves as an effective ice-breaker. And, as each selected text is complex and rich, the question that is selected or provided as the opening question may draw from or refer to any place in the text. As the class responds to the opening question and the dialogue moves forward, many other issues in the text will emerge.

There is not a single theme or a single issue in any text, and neither is there one and only one opening question. There are many possible questions, and any one of them can lead students into and through the fabric of the text.

Here are two helpful suggestions in considering or framing the opening question:

- Keep it brief and honest, and
- Make sure it is a real concern for the person who is asking it.

Once begun, the discussion will have a life of its own, and the opening question may soon be absorbed by the other questions that will flow out of the dialogue.

Context for Discussion

The purpose of Touchstones overall is to engage the discussion participants in collaborative exploration—to think critically, to analyze concepts, and to share leadership and the responsibility for our community. Engaging in constructive dialogue, critical thinking, analyzing, and being responsible are all behaviors and skills learned through regular practice. They are skills that each of us needs. Consequently, discussions that are held regularly—perhaps once a week or twice a month—quickly and reliably effect the most positive outcomes.

As the issues in the Touchstones texts concern us all, we should not and do not need to turn to experts for answers. We all know something about wanting revenge, or loneliness, or what it feels like when someone is compassionate. We all have something worthwhile to contribute to discussions of these questions, but none of us has the answer. Therefore, when we learn to listen to everyone—and to accept criticism from everyone—we start to use and build on the thoughts of others. Together, we create bridges of understanding, think seriously without reaching definite conclusions, and relate particular experiences to general concepts.

Organization of the Room

Whenever possible, the chairs or desks should be moved into a circle or around a large table in advance of starting a Touchstones discussion. This configuration allows everyone to see and hear each other and facilitates balanced engagement. In addition, the circular arrangement hinders side conversations. Nothing damages a discussion more than a few people whispering while someone else is bravely trying to explore beliefs or respond to someone else's contribution. When these inappropriate private exchanges occur, trust diminishes significantly and we all become unwilling to take risks publicly. Remember that a discussion on Touchstones texts requires cooperation, courage, and mutual respect. This is what is involved in taking responsibility for oneself and for a class.

As you and your class gain experience with Touchstones discussions, you will no longer be a simple collection of individuals. Instead, the group will become a true community—one that is thoughtfully engaged in the exploration and meaningful activity of community service.

Howard Zeiderman
Geoffrey Comber
David Townsend
Stefanie Takacs

Foreword
by Kathleen Kennedy Townsend

Reflecting on Service

Stand in front of a fire. Feel the heat. Gasp for breath, and then ask yourself whether a fireman goes into a burning building for mere money.

Now reflect that the majority of firemen in this country are volunteers.

On Memorial Day, look at the veterans who have lost part of their bodies or their youth on a foreign field. Was that a smart career move?

Our nation relies on the character of our people for its strength. To be truly self-governing we need people who are self-reliant, moral, capable of making tough decisions, and willing to serve. At our best, we teach the young to care for others, their parents, and their children. We hope others, in turn, will be good to them and care for their parents and children. Thus we create a strong nation and develop the habits of personal and social responsibility.

In 1985, Maryland became the first state requiring local school systems to offer credit to students who perform community service. Students in schools all across the state are pinpointing needs and developing innovative solutions. Like thousands of students across the nation, Maryland students are tutoring younger students in English, math, and science. They have weather-stripped and rehabilitated houses, and tended animals in the zoo. They have planted sea grasses to save our waterways, and tested pollutants in our streams. They have acted as peer counselors, created plays about drug and alcohol abuse, and entertained senior citizens with songs and fashion shows. They have been huggers at Special Olympics, and they have served meals at shelters for the homeless. These are not simply nice things to do. They develop the character necessary for a vibrant national life.

For instance, at Southern High School in Baltimore City, students tutor, visit nursing homes, and work at the Science Center. Towards the end of last semester, students spoke of their experiences. "Now I come to school because I feel that I am needed." They explained that they are much more sympathetic towards their teachers once they see how demanding teaching is— "It's tough!" The students became more responsible and more understanding of the duties adults bear.

One class in Suitland High School in Prince George's County identified the chronic lateness which caused many of the peers trouble in school. They developed questionnaires to pinpoint the reason for the lateness. Armed with the facts, they invented some innovative solutions and some obvious ones such as a daily wakeup call. Not only did eighty-seven percent of those who participated avoid suspension, but the peer counselors who had identified a disturbing issue, planned a line of attack, and then followed through, learned a lesson in effective action. As one peer counselor explained, "I learned how to solve problems."

In Charles County, students organized and operated a successful fund drive for the United Way. "They went beyond all our expectations," said John Bloom, the Superintendent, "and they learned just how competent they are. Now they are ready to take on much tougher tasks. It's great." They have gained confidence and self-esteem.

In Havre de Grace, as in many high schools, students work with mentally handicapped children. "How can I complain about not having a car?" said one. Many others saw that Special Olympians are not so different. "They also like to compete and win." These students learned to empathize with those different from themselves.

Those who tutor others see their own test scores rise. Rudy Perpich, former governor of Minnesota, is a strong advocate of community service tutoring programs as a teacher recruitment tool. He finds that a significantly higher percentage of those who tutor consider teaching as a career.

Finally, service teaches citizenship.

"Why should I care about those who live in the city?" asked one young woman who lived in a comfortable suburb. A little earlier in the same public high school, but in a different class, one young man replied to my pitch for literacy tutors, "Mrs. Townsend, what's in it for me?"

Words alone are not an effective rebuttal to the young man or woman who prefers not to get involved. The experiences of their classmates who have worked in homeless shelters, been huggers at the Special Olympics, or participated in literacy programs will confront their peers' selfishness.

One young man in the back of the class, whose teacher told me afterwards never speaks, challenged his peers, "What do you think you will do when you graduate: put up a white picket fence and close off the rest of the world? Well, it won't work."

The fundamental question remains: What do we want? If we want our children to develop fortitude and strength of character, then it is up to us to overcome the feelings of timidity and futility which thwart efforts to develop community service programs. We celebrate Rev. Martin Luther King, Jr.'s commitment to service each year, but more and more we find a need and a desire to support our communities each day.

The young have enormous talents, imagination, and energy which they will put to good use if only they are asked to help others. Dorothy Day once said that it was difficult to teach people to be virtuous, but one could create the structure in which it would be easier to do good. A program of community service gives students the opportunity to use their talents, energy, and intelligence to help others.

Still, unreflective action is sufficient to create a citizenry able and willing to make wise choices. For that, reading and thinking are necessary.

The following readings have been selected because they raise enduring human concerns. With these readings students are provided a tool with which to understand and speak about the issues that they confront. Too often, students in community service programs can only say, "It makes me feel good to help another." They cannot articulate why they may feel good, nor why that feeling may be fundamental to being truly human.

Certainly the experience of community service helps students know the happiness that comes from helping others. But it is the discussion with texts that enriches the experience by providing a way to think about and understand what they have done.

A Word about the Readings

These readings are divided into different subheadings reflecting the reasons for the reading. Thus the readings in the chapters entitled "Preparation" and "Historical" should be studied prior to the actual community service. The historical readings anchor service or volunteering within the American tradition, while the other readings demonstrate that the question of how to be a citizen has fascinated and disturbed thinkers since people began to write.

The section entitled "General Reflections on Service" consists of readings which would be appropriate for whatever service the student undertakes. Following this general reflection section are four chapters where the readings would be more appropriate to the actual service performed. Politics raises questions about the nature of a state and the use of power. Students who are engaged in a political campaign or a particular issue can see how others have thought about many of the issues that they are now confronting.

Similarly, the sections on tutoring, peer counseling, and the aged draw on the writings of those familiar with the issues that may be raised through performing service in these areas.

Clearly, this is not a comprehensive anthology. Each community service teacher will have a wealth of his or her own favorite readings to draw upon.

At a time when the young feel encouraged and mobilized by the changes around them, the simple acts will reinforce their confidence and the courage to try something even more difficult. This is crucial. "Courage," as Winston Churchill said, "is the most important virtue, for it is the one virtue which makes all others possible."

The young have enormous talent, intelligence, and enthusiasm. They will put it to good use and make a real contribution to their communities if only they are asked and shown a way. Now is the time to ask.

Unit I
Preparation for Service

Passers-by
Franz Kafka

When you go walking at night up a street and a man, visible a long way off—for the street goes uphill and there is a full moon—comes running toward you, well, you don't catch hold of him as he passes. You let him run on even if he is a feeble old man, even if someone is chasing him and yelling at him. For it is night, and you can't help it if the street goes uphill in the moonlight. And besides, these two have maybe started a chase to amuse themselves, or perhaps they are both chasing a third person, or perhaps the first is an innocent man and the second wants to murder him and so you would become an accessory, or they are merely running separately home to bed, or perhaps the first has a gun. And anyhow, haven't you a right to be tired; haven't you been drinking a lot of wine? You're thankful they are now both long out of sight.

Life of Pericles
Plutarch

Augustus Caesar, Emperor of Rome, once saw some wealthy foreigners fondly holding puppies in their arms. Shocked, he asked whether women in their country had stopped having children. By this remark, the emperor was criticizing people who spend their kindness and affection on animals instead of on their own kind. In a similar way, we criticize those who misuse the natural love of inquiry and observation. Most people observe and listen to what isn't worth their attention. They neglect things which are excellent in themselves and which might do them some good.

Our outward senses, our eyes and ears, respond to whatever strikes them. But with our inward senses, our minds and souls, we can choose. We have the power to direct ourselves to what we decide. So it becomes our duty to study and observe the very best objects. Not only are they worth thinking about—they may also improve us. It is just like in the case of colors. A fresh and pleasant color stimulates and strengthens the sight. So a person should focus his mind on what pleases it, strengthens it, and attracts it to its own good and advantage. For the mind, such objects are acts of virtue. When people see virtuous acts or read about them, they produce in our minds an eagerness to imitate them or even to do better.

In most things or actions we like, we don't feel a desire to imitate it. Many times, in fact, we may be pleased with an object but scorn the person who made it. This happens with things like perfumes, beautiful dyes, or delicious food. We enjoy the product, but feel superior to the maker. There is an interesting story about Alexander the Great which illustrates this point. King Philip listened to his son Alexander play the flute with great skill. The king enjoyed the piece but turned to his son and said, "Aren't you ashamed to play so well? A king should be able to enjoy music, he should not be able to play it."

Even with great works of art, something similar is true. No person looking at the great statue of Jupiter by the famous sculptor Phidias ever desired to become another Phidias. For it doesn't follow that if a work pleases us by its beauty, the person who made it deserves our admiration. That's why these things really bring no great gain to the viewers. For on seeing them we don't desire to do the same thing. But virtue and nobility and honor and goodness are quite different. Even a mere account or story of them can so affect our minds that we admire the actions and want to imitate those who did them. We long to possess and enjoy money, power, and expensive homes, but we ourselves want to act courageously and nobly. We can quickly see the difference between these two kinds of things. We are quite content to be given money and expensive goods by others. But we want others to experience virtuous acts of our doing. Actions of this kind and moral good itself provoke us to actions of our own.

The Ethics
Aristotle

A man is thought to be great who thinks that he is worthy of great things and *is* worthy of them. If a man thinks that he is worthy of great things but is not, then he is only a fool. Self-esteem is connected to greatness, and a great person knows he deserves to be honored by others.

A truly great man must be the best in every way. For example, it would be wrong for a great man to run from danger, or to do wrong to someone else.

The great man is mostly concerned with honors, but only if they are given by good men. He will despise honors given by men who are less, good or bad, and honors given for petty reasons. He will not care much about wealth and power, and he won't be overjoyed at good luck, or depressed if things go bad. So you can see why great men are thought to be proud. But some men are proud without having a right to be. They are only imitating what great men are, but are not themselves really great.

The great man likes to give favors, but he is ashamed of receiving them. To give is the mark of a superior person, and to have a favor done to you is to be inferior. The great man will forget or ignore favors done to him but will remember those he does to others.

The great man won't do many things, because not very many things are worthy of him. But the things he does, he will do excellently, and they will be great things. He will never do anything secretly, nor hide his true feelings. This is what cowards do. So he always tells the truth. He has very few friends. Friends should be equals, and very few people are his equals. He doesn't praise or blame people. He would only praise people and their acts if they were better than his. On the other hand, he expects everyone else to behave worse, so why blame them?

Finally, a great man will walk slowly and speak evenly and in a low tone—for to walk quickly and to speak unevenly and in a high tone are signs that you are excited and out of control. A great man thinks there is nothing about which one should get excited and worried.

Such, then, is the great man.

Causes of Unhappiness
Blaise Pascal

Even as children we are told to take care of our reputations, our property, and our friends. We are even told to look after the reputations and property of our friends. We are given chores and homework and are constantly told that we will not be happy unless both we and our friends have health, good reputations, and money in the bank. If one thing goes wrong, we are told we will be unhappy. So, from the first moment of each day we are burdened with responsibilities.

You will say that this is a strange way to make people happy. Could one even imagine a better way to make them unhappy? But what should one do? If you took people's worries away they would be forced to look at themselves. They would have to think about what they are, where they come from, and where they are going. For many, these thoughts would be unbearable. This is why people have to keep busy. Even when they have free time, they are advised to spend it keeping busy with sports and hobbies. Isn't such a person's heart empty and ugly?

The Writings of Mencius

Mencius said, "Everyone has a heart that is sensitive to the sufferings of others. The great kings of the past had this sort of sensitive heart and thus adopted compassionate policies. Bringing order to the realm is as easy as moving an object in your palm when you have a sensitive heart and put into practice compassionate policies.

Let me give an example of what I mean when I say everyone has a heart that is sensitive to the sufferings of others Anyone today who suddenly saw a baby about to fall into a well would feel alarmed and concerned. It would not be because he wanted to improve his relations with the child's parents, nor because he wanted a good reputation among his friends and neighbors, nor because he disliked hearing the child cry.

From this, it follows that anyone who lacks feelings of commiseration, shame, and courtesy or a sense of right and wrong is not a human being. From the feeling of commiseration, benevolence grows; from the feeling of shame, righteousness grows; from the feeling of courtesy, ritual grows; from a sense of right and wrong, wisdom grows.

People have these four germs, just as they have four limbs. For someone with these four potentials to claim incompetence is to cripple himself; to say his ruler is incapable of them is to cripple his ruler. Those who know how to develop the four potentials within themselves will take off like a fire or burst forth like a spring. Those who can fully develop them can protect the entire land while those unable to develop them cannot even take care of their parents."

On the Human Soul: Cures for Sadness
St. Thomas Aquinas

Question: Are there any human cures for sadness?

Answer: There are some sorrows that only God can take away. Still, human beings were made to be happy. They were not made to be sad. So there are things human beings can do to cure sadness. Here are five cures for sadness:

1. Any delightful activity—for sadness is to the soul as weariness is to the body. Delightful activity is like rest for the soul.
2. Tears.
3. The compassion of friends.
4. Learning what is true about the world—this seems to help some people more than it helps others.
5. Bathing and sleeping—for when your body feels better, your soul will feel better too.

To say more about the third point, let me ask whether the compassion of friends is a cure for sadness. Some people don't think so. Here are some arguments.

1. It would seem that sadness isn't cured by the compassion of friends. As St. Augustine says, "When many people are celebrating together, the pleasure of each one is greater than it would be if each were alone." In the same way, when many people are sad together, the sadness of each is greater than it would be if each were alone.

2. Friends, as St. Augustine says, repay love with love. But a friend who is being compassionate because of his friend's sadness also himself becomes sad. His sadness makes the friend he was trying to cure even sadder. Therefore, the compassion of friends is not a cure for sadness.

On the other hand, I say that everyone knows from experience that when we are sad, the compassion of friends helps. Aristotle says that there are two reasons for this. First, sadness is like a weight which we are carrying. When friends are being compassionate, they are helping us to carry this weight. They are making it lighter for us.

Aristotle's second reason is even better. When a person's friends share his sadness, that person sees that his friends love him. This fact is a source of pleasure. But pleasure, as we have already said, eases pain. It follows, therefore, that sadness is eased when friends share it.

My answers to the two arguments above are the following:

1. When a person shares in our joy or in our sadness, he is showing friendship. In both cases friendship gives us pleasure. It is this pleasure which helps to take away sadness.

2. It is true that a friend's sadness, because of our sadness, adds to our sadness. However, there is also pleasure, because we realize that the friend loves us.

A Sunday Evening Talk
Booker T. Washington

The old idea about this life was that it was something to be gotten rid of as soon as possible. It was something to be shaken off. It wasn't connected in any large degree with the life that is to come. More and more we are learning, however, a new idea of life—that each of us is a continuous being. The life in this world is as important as the life in the next world. We simply continue to live after we pass from this stage of being into another stage of being. In a word, the idea is becoming more and more emphasized that this life is something to be made great, something to be improved.

I believe that it is impossible for a person to live a high life— a noble life in the future world—who does not live a noble life in this world. I don't believe those individuals who are mean, low, and ungrateful in this life are transferred into another life and made higher beings. I believe, very much, that in another life we are what we are in this life. We are certainly preparing ourselves here for what we are to be in another life. So we should practice the habit, day by day, of trying to get all we can out of life. Be sure we get the best things in this life, be sure we learn to do the best things in this life, be sure we learn the higher things in this life.

The person who has learned to love trees, to love flowers, or has learned to get enjoyment and pleasure out of rain—out of everything that is put here by our Creator for our enjoyment—is a person who is happy and contented. Perhaps there are many things we have not yet discovered, but I do not believe there is a thing put on this earth that is not meant for our use—to give us enjoyment and comfort. The more we learn to love trees, the more we learn to love sunshine and rain, the more we learn to get out of nature, the nobler we shall grow day by day.

And so, I want you to get the idea that each day brings to you a serious responsibility. You should try to get as much out of the twenty-four hours as possible. Learn to get out of every hour, every year, as much as is possible for you to get. You have only one life to live. Remember you pass through this life but once, and if you fail, you fail perhaps for all time. You should consider closely the serious obligation you have upon you to live properly through a day, through a year, and you should try to get everything that is best out of that day, out of that year.

Suppose you have only a dollar to spend during the year. Would you spend every cent during the first six months? Now, you have only one life that you may shape as you will. You will not have it tomorrow again. How careful then you should think about how to spend each moment, each hour, each day of your life!

My experience has been that one gets out of life what he puts in it. If he puts hard, earnest study and effort into his life, he gets pleasure, satisfaction, and enjoyment out of it. As I have said, if an individual puts hard, earnest work into his life, he will get strength out of it. On the other hand, if he is indifferent and reckless, you will find him continually complaining, finding fault, seeking another place. You will find such an individual unhappy, and at the same time, making everyone about him unhappy too. He is simply living on the outer edges of his work, instead of entering into the life of it.

An individual gets happiness out of his study or work in proportion to how much hard, earnest work he puts into it. Suppose you find a person who is constantly complaining that the world has no love in it. You will also find an individual who is cold and hard-hearted himself. He doesn't love the people in the world—he is not loved by the other people. He gets out of life just what he puts into it. Suppose you find someone constantly complaining that those around him are selfish and cold in their treatment of him. Examine into the cause of that individual's complaint. You will find that he is cold and selfish himself. We get out of every part of life just about what we put into it.

Life should give us the opportunity for the highest mental, physical, and spiritual enjoyment. The old idea that people used to believe, and still believe, is that in order to get happiness, one must punish the physical part of oneself. This idea has largely passed away. Out of earth, out of nature, out of everything with which we come into contact, we should learn to get the highest physical, mental, and spiritual enjoyment. We would then learn to look at life in the right way.

Philanthropy
Henry David Thoreau

I confess that in the past I have indulged very little in philanthropic and charitable activities. There are those who have used all their arts to persuade me to undertake the support of a poor family in town. If I had nothing to do I might try my hand at such a pastime, for the devil finds work for the idle. However, whenever I have given myself over to such work and even made the offer to such people, they have all without hesitation preferred to remain poor. While my townsmen and women devote themselves in so many ways to the good of their fellows, I trust that at least one person in this town may be spared to pursue other and less humane pursuits.

You must have a special talent for charity as well as for any other job. And yet doing good is one of the professions which is filled with workers. Moreover, I have tried it honestly, and, strange as it may seem, I am satisfied that it does not agree with my nature. But I would not stand between any man and his talents. To him who does this work with his whole heart, soul, and life, which I decline, I would say: Persevere, even if everyone calls it evil, as it is most likely they will.

However, be sure you give the poor the aid they most need, though it be your example which leaves them far behind. If you give them money, exert yourself in the spending of it and do not just give it to them. We make curious mistakes sometimes. Often the poor man is not so much cold and hungry as he is dirty and ragged. It is partly his taste and his own judgment that he lives a certain way and not simply through misfortune. If all you do is give him money, he would not know better and would merely buy more rags with it.

There are a thousand men and women cutting at the branches of evil to one who is striking at the root. It may be that he who bestows the largest amount of time and money on the needy and poor is doing the most to produce the very misery which he strives in vain to relieve. It is like the pious slave-breeder who devotes the profits from the sale of every tenth slave to buy a day off for the rest. Some show kindness to the poor by giving them work in their kitchens. Would they not do better if they worked there themselves?

I believe that what most saddens the reformer and do-gooder is not his sympathy with his fellows in distress. Rather, even if he is the holiest son of God, he is instead saddened by his own private distress. If this were changed, if springtime came to him, he would forsake his charitable work and his generous companions without apology or excuse. My excuse for not doing good to others by lecturing against the use of tobacco is that I never used it myself. That is a penalty which reformed tobacco-users have to pay. If you should ever fall into one of these philanthropies or ways of helping others, don't let your left hand know what your right hand does. For it is not worth knowing. Rescue the drowning and keep your own shoestrings tied. Take your time about things, and set yourself to do some work.

Our way of life has been corrupted by communication with holy people and saints. Our hymnbooks are filled with a melodious cursing of God and enduring him forever. One would have to say that even the prophets and redeemers had rather consoled our fears than confirmed and encouraged our hopes. Nowhere is there recorded a simple and irrepressible satisfaction with the gift of life, which would be truly a memorable praise of God. All health and success do me good, however far away they appear. All disease and failure help to make me sad and do me evil, however much sympathy we have with them. If, then, we would indeed restore mankind, let us first be as simple and well as Nature ourselves. We should dispel the clouds and anguish which hang over our own brows, and take up a little life into our pores. Do not stay to be an overseer of the poor; attempt to become one of the worthy people of the world.

The Rights of Women
Mary Wollstonecraft

Mental activity, like bodily activity, is at first difficult and unpleasant. Therefore, many people let others both work and think for them. When in a group, if a person asserts an opinion with great heat, very often it is a prejudice. Generally such a person has a high respect for the opinions of some relative or friend without fully understanding the opinions which he is now so eager to have us also believe. Therefore, he holds these opinions with a degree of force which would surprise even the person who held them in the first place.

It is now fashionable to respect prejudices. When we dare to face our prejudices, motivated by feeling of humanity and armed with reason, we are often asked whether our ancestors, who created these opinions, were fools. I reply that they weren't. Our ancestors' opinions were all probably thought about and based on some reason. But often the reason they had was special and useful only at that time. It was not a fundamental principle that would be reasonable at all times.

Our ancestors' old and moss-covered opinions become prejudices when *we* lazily accept them, only because these opinions have been with us for a long time. An opinion is a prejudice when it is one which we like and hold strongly, but for which we can give no reason. The moment a reason can be given for an opinion, it stops being a prejudice, though it may still be a mistake or an error. This way of arguing, if we can call it arguing, reminds me of what is crudely and vulgarly called "a woman's reason." For women sometimes say they love someone or believe certain things *just because* they love or believe them, and they can't or won't give any reasons.

It is useless to talk with people who only use affirmatives and negatives, who say either "yes" or "no" to everything. Before you can bring yourself or someone else to a point where you can begin a useful discussion, you must go back to the simple principles which precede the prejudices. And it is ten to one that you will be stopped as you try to do this. You will even be told that, though these simple principles are true in theory, they are false in practice. When you hear this from people, you may infer that their reason has whispered some doubts to them. For it generally happens that people assert their opinions with the greatest heat when they begin to waver and have doubts about them. They then try to drive out their own doubts by convincing their opponents, and grow angry when their own doubts continue to bother and haunt them.

THIS PAGE MAY NOT BE REPRODUCED
OR DISPLAYED IN ANY FORM.

Cassandra
Florence Nightingale

Give us back our suffering, suffering rather than indifference. For out of nothing comes nothing, but out of our suffering may come a cure. Better to have pain than paralysis. A hundred people struggle and drown in the waves at the shore, one discovers the new world. Rather, ten times rather, die in the surf, showing the way to a new world, than stand idly by on the far shore.

Look at that lizard. "It is not hot," he says, "I like the heat. The temperature which destroys you is life to me." Similarly, the state of society about which some complain, makes others happy. Why should those who suffer complain to those who are happy? The happy do not suffer. They would not understand the complaints any more than the lizard would understand the sufferings of a sheep in the heat.

The changing world is necessarily divided into two classes. There are those who are born to the best of what there is and enjoy it. On the other hand, there are those who wish for something different and better, and try to create it. Without both these classes, the world would be badly off. Both classes are the very conditions of progress. Were no people discontented with what they have, the world would never change and reach anything better. And through the other class, a balance is secured. By enjoying the best of what is created, these good things which have been made are retained for the world. And we must not quarrel with either class for not possessing the privileges of the other. The laws of nature for each make that impossible.

Is being discontent a privilege? Yes, it is a privilege for you to suffer for your class—a privilege not reserved for the Redeemer and the martyrs alone. It is a privilege enjoyed by large numbers in every age. But the commonplace life of thousands has little interest because it is merely a common suffering. It is the story of those who do not have the courage either to fight against and resist or to accept the civilization of their times as the other classes do.

Unit II

Historical Perspectives on Service

A Model of Christian Charity
John Winthrop

God Almighty in His most holy ways and wisdom has set down the condition of all mankind that at all times there must be some who will be rich, some poor; some who will be great in power and position, others who will be poor, weak, and lowly.

One of the reasons for this is that, in this way, every person will have a need for each other. The rich need the poor, and the poor need the rich, so that the whole society might be more closely knit together in the bond of brotherly love. From this, it follows plainly that no man is made more honorable or wealthy than another for his own sake or in respect to his own worth. Rather, this order of things is for the glory of his Creator and the common good of mankind. It is for this reason that God calls wealth *His* gold and silver, etc. He claims all the use of gold and silver as *His* due. "Honor the Lord with your riches." Since God has ranked all men into two sorts—rich and poor—the rich are those who can live comfortably by their own means, and the poor live according to how the rich distribute the goods.

There are two roles by which we should treat one another: justice and mercy. Justice and mercy can be distinguished in actions and in goals. Sometimes they can occur together. For example, if you show mercy to a rich man who is in great trouble, or by doing simple plain justice to a poor man with regard to some particular contract.

Similarly, there is a double law which should order our dealings with one another—the law of nature and the law of grace, or, the moral law and the law of the Gospel. By the law of nature or the moral law, man is commanded to love his neighbor as himself. This law concerns all our dealings with our fellow men. To apply this to the works of mercy, this law demands two things: first, that every person offer help to another who needs help; second, that he does this act of kindness out of the same love and affection he has for his own welfare.

The law of grace or the law of the Gospel is different from the law of nature or the moral law. First, though the law of nature was given to mankind by God, it can be known by *all men*, whether they are Christian or not. The law of the Gospel or of grace is only given to those who have faith as a Christian. Second, the law of nature binds one man to another under God, but the law of the Gospel or grace makes those who have faith to be brothers in Christ also. This puts a difference between Christians and other people. Third, the law of nature gives no rules for dealing with enemies but the Gospel commands us to love our enemies. Proof: "If your enemy is hungry, feed him; love your enemies, do good to them that hate you" (Matthew 5:44).

This law of the Gospel demands even more. There is a time when a Christian, though he has not given all he has, must nevertheless give more than his inclinations dictate. He must perform some extraordinary service. But there is also a time when a Christian must sell *all* he has and give to the poor as they did in the apostles' time.

Bonifacius: Essays to Do Good
Cotton Mather

I think this enthusiasm should be carried into our neighborhood. Neighbors! You are connected one to another. And the way you behave should make everyone in the neighborhood glad to live there. We read: "A righteous person is better than his neighbor." But we don't think so, unless he is better *as* a neighbor. He must excel in being a good neighbor.

First: the poor people who lie wounded must have their wounds cared for and healed. A modern prince was recently told: "To be in need is to deserve your favor. Good neighbor, put on that royal quality! See who in the neighborhood may deserve your favor." We are told: "This is pure religion—to pay visits to the widows in their need, and to those who have no father." The orphans and widows, and all children in need of help should be visited and given the help they need.

Neighbors! Care for the orphans and widows in your neighborhood. They meet great difficulties, and are often tempted to do wrong. While their relatives were alive, they may have been poorly provided for, but at least they had something. How much worse off must they be now that they are alone? Think about it, and this should be the result: "I helped the children who had no helper, and caused the widow to sing with joy." In this way, each and every person in the neighborhood is thought about. Would it be too much for you at least once a week to think: "Which of my neighbors is reduced to penny-pinching and painful poverty?" Think: "Who is heartbroken with a sad death in the family?" And think: "Which neighbor's soul is being tempted to evil, or being hurt in some way?" But then think: "What shall be done for such neighbors?"

First: you will pity them. "Have compassion for one another— be pitiful." This has always been and always will be justly expected of you. And let our pity for them burst out into a prayer for them. It would be a fine practice for you in your private daily prayers to think: "What misery have I seen today that I may do well now to ask for the mercy of the Lord."

But this is not all. Probably, you should visit them; and when you visit, comfort them. Carry to them some good word that may make their sad heart more glad.

And lastly: give them assistance that will help them in their misery. Assist them with advice, assist them with greetings from other people. If it is necessary, give them what they need: "Give bread to the hungry; offer them shelter in your house; give clothes to those who are naked or in rags." At least, I beg of you: "If you have nothing else to give to the poor and wretched, give a tear or two for their misery." This is better than nothing.

As you consider what helps make a good neighborhood, the main principle I would have you keep in mind is that you look to the spiritual needs of your neighborhood as well as the material needs. Be concerned that lies and temptations do not make your neighbors commit sins. If there are lazy persons, I beg you, cure them of their idleness. Find them work; set them to work; keep them to work.

If any children are not getting an education, don't allow that to go on. Let care be taken that they may be better educated and taught to read, taught their religion and the truths and actions of our Lord and Savior.

One more thing: if anyone in the neighborhood has bad habits—lovingly but faithfully point this out to them. If any in the neighborhood are hurting themselves or their families—carefully point this out to them. If there are families who do not pray, never stop urging them until you have persuaded them actively to worship God. If there is any service of God or of His people that is needed, tenderly urge it to be done. Whenever you see someone being trapped in some way, be so kind as to tell him of the danger and save him. By putting good books into your neighbors' hands and getting them to promise to read them, who can tell what good you may do to them!

Man the Reformer

Ralph Waldo Emerson

What is a man born for except to be a Reformer, a Re-maker of what man has made, a renouncer of lies, a restorer of truth and goodness, copying the good things which Nature places around us all? Let man renounce everything which is not true to him, and make sure that all he does is backed by firm reasons. He should do nothing for which he does not have a world of reason.

The power, which is the motive for all efforts to reform, is faith in Man. The Reformer must be convinced that there is an infinite worth in all men. All particular acts of reform are the removing of something which prevents a man's true self from appearing. Is it not our highest duty to honor the humanness in us? I ought not to allow any man to feel rich in my presence because he owns much land. I ought to make him feel that I can do without his wealth, that I cannot be bought. Even though I might have no money and might even receive bread from him, he is still the poor man beside me. And if a woman or child tells me of a feeling or thought which is more just and right than my feelings or thoughts, I should respect them and admit them to be better than mine, even if they change my whole way of life.

Americans have many virtues, but they do not have Faith and Hope. Americans misunderstand these two words more than any others. Americans have no Faith. They rely on the power of the dollar; they are dead to feelings and sentiments. But if I talk with a sincere wise man or with a poet, I see what one brave man might do. If I talk with an honest young person who still has his own wild untamed thoughts, who has not been spoiled by the unbelievers and their schools and other institutions, I see what one great thought carried out into practice might do.

I see now why the practical man distrusts theories; it is because he can't see *how* they work. Look, he scoffs, at the tools you have to make this fine new world of yours. How, he asks, can we ever make that new world you want out of foolish, sick, and selfish men and women, such as we know people to be? But the believer, the man with Faith and Hope, not only believes his heaven to be possible, but already is beginning to exist. It will not exist with the men, women, and things used by the statesman and politician. It will exist with men and women changed and raised above themselves by the power of principles. Principles make it possible to rise up above things which are only practical.

It is the sentiment of love which is the cure of all ills. If we love, then immediately what was impossible becomes possible. Our age and history for a thousand years has not been an age of kindness; it has been a history of selfishness. Our distrust of everyone is very expensive. By distrust we make thieves and burglars. By our law courts and jails we keep them so. If we accepted the feeling of love for some reasonable period, the criminal and outcast would be brought to our side in tears, devoted to helping us in any way he can.

Look at this society of ours with its working men and women. We let ourselves be served by these workers, but we live apart from them and meet them in the streets almost without seeing them. We do not praise their skills, nor are we happy if they have good luck, nor do we encourage their hopes, nor vote in their interests. Thus we play the part of the selfish lord and king who has existed from the beginning of the world.

Let our love flow out to our fellows. In one day, it would work the greatest revolution of them all. The state must consider the poor man, and everyone must speak for him. Every child that is born must have a fair chance for an honest living. Let your laws be improved by the generosity of the rich and not by the demands of the poor. Let us learn the habit of giving. Let us understand that fair rules come from no one taking more than his share, however rich he might be. I must see that the world is better for me living here and find my reward in the act. Love would put a new face on this weary old world where we live as enemies. Love would over-come vain politicians; it would show how powerless armies and navies are. One day all men will learn to love, and every evil will be dissolved in universal sunshine.

Democracy in America
Alexis de Tocqueville

Americans form associations to build churches, to give entertainment, to write and sell books, to send missionaries overseas, to construct hotels and colleges. Whenever in France some new task is undertaken it is always by the government; in America you will find an association of people doing that job.

I met several kinds of associations in America that I had never even dreamed of before. And I admired the skill with which Americans managed to get a great many people to agree about a common project and then voluntarily to work on it together.

I have traveled around England also, from which Americans took many laws and customs, but the skill of forming associations and groups is not used nearly so much there. The English perform great things singly—one person alone—whereas the Americans form associations to carry out the smallest purposes. It is clear that the English consider associations as powerful means to do some things, but Americans regard it as the *only* way to do some things. Is it just an accident that the most democratic country on the face of the earth is the country where they have perfected the art of pursuing common objects in association together? Is there any necessary connection between the principle of forming associations and the principle of equality?

Aristocratic societies always contain a great number of powerful and wealthy citizens among a great multitude of people who are, by themselves, powerless. Each of the powerful and wealthy men can achieve great tasks single-handedly. In aristocratic societies, men don't need to combine together to act because they are already strongly held together. In a way, every powerful and wealthy citizen is already the head of a permanent and compulsory association, an association where many powerless citizens are dependent on the powerful and wealthy citizen and must carry out his plans.

In a democracy, on the other hand, all the citizens are weak and independent by themselves. They can't do much of anything alone. They all remain weak and powerless if they do not learn to cooperate and help one another willingly.

It is easy for several people in an aristocracy to work together because they already know each other, understand each other, and fix the rules of working together. In a democracy, members of an association must be very numerous to have any power. My fellow Frenchmen are not bothered by this. They believe that the weaker and more incompetent the citizens become, the more able and active the government should become, so that society at large may do what individual citizens can no longer do. They think this answers the whole problem, but I think they are wrong.

A government can do a *part* of what *some* of the largest of the American corporations and several states have already tried. But what government could ever do the huge number of small tasks which American citizens do every day by forming their groups? It is easy to foresee that the time is getting near when a man alone will be less and less able to produce the most common necessities of life. The task of government will then constantly increase, and it will grow greater every day. The more government grows instead of forming associations, the more individual citizens will need the assistance of government and will therefore lose their ideas of forming associations. These are causes and effects which constantly create one another. Will the government of a country ultimately take on the management of everything which no single citizen can do for himself? If the government ever wholly took over the place of private companies, the morals and intelligence of a democratic people would be as much in danger as its manufacturing companies and businesses.

Only by means of social influences of men upon one another can the human mind and feelings and opinions and heart be developed. I have shown that these influences are, by nature, almost nil in democratic countries. Therefore, they must be artificially created by forming groups and associations.

"True and False Philanthropy"
from McGuffey's Reader

Mr. Fantom: I despise a narrow field. O, for the reign of universal goodness. I want to make everyone good and happy.

Mr. Goodman: That would be a big job. Don't you think you should start with a town or neighborhood first?

Mr. Fantom: Sir, I have a plan in my head for relieving the miseries of the whole world. As it is, everything is bad. I would change all the laws and put an end to all wars. There would no longer be any punishments, and I would free all prisoners. That's what I call doing things on a large scale.

Mr. Goodman: You sure would be. As to releasing prisoners, I don't like that very much. You would free a few criminals, and all honest men would pay. As to the rest of your plan, it would help if all countries became Christian. Yet, there would still be misery enough left since God meant that this world should be earth and not heaven. And, sir, among all your changes, you must first destroy human corruption before you can make the world as perfect as you pretend.

Mr. Fantom: Your project would reinforce the chains which my project is meant to break.

Mr. Goodman: I have no projects. People who are restless, idle, and vain give birth to projects and schemes. I am too busy for projects and great plans, too satisfied for vast theories, and too honest and humble to be a philosopher. What I hope for right now is to fix the wrongs of one poor worker who was harmed by his employer. Then I hope to investigate a man who let someone in his care fall into poverty. And I hope you'll help me.

Mr. Fantom: Let the city help you. Don't ask for my help in such small problems. The wrongs suffered by Poles and South Americans fill my mind. I don't have time to bother with the problems of just one worker. The goodness of philosophers fixes on empires and continents. Anyone can do some small good by his neighbor. A philosopher spreads light and knowledge to the whole world.

Mr. Goodman: You're remarkable. You love mankind so dearly and yet avoid all opportunities to do anyone some good. You have a noble desire to help millions and yet feel so little compassion for individual people. You long to free empires, and yet you refuse to teach your own town and comfort your own family. But come and help me get the old people who live here a little bit more to eat.

Mr. Fantom: Sir, my mind is too busy with what's happening in Europe and Poland to bring it down to something so small. I despise the person whose goodness is exhausted in the concerns of his own family or city or country.

Mr. Goodman: I'd be quite happy to help a Pole or a South American, but I'd sooner help someone I know in my own town. One must begin to love somewhere, and I think it is natural to love one's own family and do good in one's own neighborhood as anywhere else. If everyone in every family, village, and county did the same, then all of these great projects and schemes would be fulfilled.

Mr. Fantom: A person of large views will always be on the lookout for great occasions to prove his goodness.

Mr. Goodman: But if these are so distant we can't reach them, or if they are so vast we can't grasp them, then we let a thousand kind, small actions slip through our fingers. So between the great thing the person you talk about cannot do, and the little things he will not do, life passes, and nothing gets done.

Charitable Effort
Jane Addams

All those hints and glimpses of a larger and more satisfying democracy, which literature and our own hopes supply, have a tendency to slip away from us. We are left sadly unguided and puzzled when we attempt to act upon them.

Our conceptions of morality, like all our other ideas, pass through a course of development. The difficulty comes in adjusting our action, which has become hardened into customs and habits, to these changing moral ideas. When this adjustment is not made, we suffer from the strain and indecision of believing one view and acting on another.

Probably there is no relation in life which our democracy is changing more rapidly than the charitable relation—that relation between benefactor and beneficiary. At the same time there is nothing in our modern experience which reveals so clearly the lack of that very equality which democracy implies. We have reached the moment when democracy has made such inroads upon this relationship that the complacency of the old-fashioned charitable man is gone forever. Yet, at the same time, the very need and existence of charity denies us the consolation and freedom which democracy will at last give.

It is quite obvious that the ethics of none of us are clearly defined, and we are continually obliged to act in circles of habit, based upon convictions which we no longer hold. Thus our estimate of the effect of environment and social conditions has doubtless altered faster than our methods of administrating charity have changed. Formerly when it was believed that poverty was synonymous with vice and laziness, and that the prosperous man was the righteous man, charity was administered harshly with a good conscience. For the charitable agent really blamed the individual for his poverty, and the very fact of his own superior prosperity gave him a feeling of superior morality.

We have learned since that time to measure by other standards and have ceased to accord exclusive respect to the money-earning capacity. While it is still rewarded out of all proportion to any other, its possession is by no means assumed to imply the possession of the highest moral qualities. We have learned to judge men by their social virtues as well as by their business capacity, by their devotion to intellectual and disinterested aims, and by their public spirit, and we naturally resent being obliged to judge poor people so solely upon their lack of wealth. Yet our democratic instinct instantly takes alarm. It is largely in this modern tendency to judge all men by one democratic standard, while the old charitable attitude commonly allowed the use of two standards, that causes much of our present difficulty. We know that unceasing labor becomes wearing and brutalizing, and our position is totally untenable if we judge large numbers of our fellows solely upon their ability to keep working.

We sometimes say that our charity is too scientific, but we would doubtless be much more correct in our estimate if we said that it is not scientific enough. We dislike arranging things merely alphabetically without indicating what is important and what is insignificant. Our feeling of revolt is probably not unlike that which afflicted the students of plants in the middle of the last century, when flowers were listed in alphabetical order. No doubt the students, wearied to death, many times said that it was all too scientific and were much perplexed and worried when they found traces of structure which their so-called scientific principles were totally unable to account for. But all this happened before science had become evolutionary science, before it had a principle of life from within. The very indications and discoveries which formerly perplexed, later illumined and made the study absorbing and alive.

We are singularly slow to apply this evolutionary principle to human affairs in general, although it is quickly being applied to the education of children. We are at last learning to follow the development of the child; to expect certain traits under certain conditions; to adapt methods and matter to his growing mind. No "advanced educator" can allow himself to be so absorbed in the question of what a child ought to be as to exclude the discovery of what he is. But in our charitable efforts we think much more of what a man ought to be than of what he is or what he may become; we ruthlessly force our conventions and standards upon him with a sternness which we would consider stupid indeed were an educator to use it in forcing his mature, intellectual convictions upon an underdeveloped mind.

Unit III

General Reflections on Service

Attitude of the Giver of Charity
The Quran (2:262-265)

Those who spend their wealth in God's cause and do not follow their spending with reminders of their benevolence or hurtful words will have their rewards with their Lord: no fear for them, nor will they grieve.

A kind word and forgiveness is better than a charitable deed followed by hurtful words: God is self-sufficient, forbearing.

You who believe, do not cancel out your charitable deeds with reminders and hurtful words, like someone who spends his wealth only to be seen by people, not believing in God and the Last Day. Such a person is like a rock with earth on it: heavy rain falls and leaves it completely bare. Such people get no rewards for their works: God does not guide the disbelievers.

But those who spend their wealth in order to gain God's approval, and as an affirmation of their own faith, are like a garden on a hill: heavy rain falls and it produces double its normal yield; even if no heavy rain falls, it will still be watered by the dew. God sees all that you do.

The Pessimist's Handbook
Arthur Schopenhauer

A man's happiness and also almost every friendship he has rest on illusion. As a rule, when he learns more about either, the happiness or friendship disappears. In spite of this, here as everywhere, people must have courage and pursue truth. They must never get tired of trying to get straight about themselves and the world. When they discover that an illusion made them happy, they should have courage and keep moving ahead. People who do this can be certain of one thing. They will never discover any worthlessness in themselves. For to feel worthless is the worst and, in fact, the only suffering.

All sufferings of the mind are healed and, in fact, immediately relieved by the firm sense of one's own worth. A person who believes in his worth can sit down quietly under the weight of terrible sufferings. Though such a person may have no pleasures, no joys, and no friends, he can rest content in himself. That's how strong a comfort can come from feeling one's own worth. It is the greatest blessing on earth. On the other hand, nothing can help a person who knows his own worthlessness. All he can do is try to hide it by deceiving other people. Or he can try to deafen them by making lots of noise. Unfortunately, neither trick can serve him for very long.

The Metaphysics of Morals
Immanuel Kant

When we can, we should give to others who are in need. It's one of our duties. We also know there are many people who give because they enjoy giving and not because it's a duty. They are pleased when they can give to others. They act without any hidden purpose such as self-interest or wanting to feel important. They are just kind, decent people. I claim there is a great difference between kind people and those who give because it's their duty. Giving because it's our duty has moral value. The same action, when done simply from kindness, has no moral worth at all. When a kind person helps another, he is only doing what he wants to do. In this action he is no different from anyone doing what he wants.

Suppose we very much want to honor someone. If it turns out to be useful to the public and in agreement with duty, it is perfectly fine to do it. Our action should be praised and encouraged. But we shouldn't be esteemed or admired for what we did. Our action lacked a real moral support. The support for our action should have been our duty, whether we felt like honoring that person or not. In the example we just gave, we *wanted* to honor someone. It just turned out to have been the right thing to do.

Take the case of a philanthropist—someone who loves others and gives money, food, or buildings to people he doesn't even know. Suppose that he feels great sorrow because of a personal loss. He no longer cares about the troubles of others because now he is so overwhelmed by his own. Yet, he is still rich and powerful enough to help others who need it. Suppose now that he tears himself away from his own pain. He gives money to others because it is his duty, and not only, as in the past, because he wanted to. Then, for the first time, his action will have real moral worth.

Take another example. Suppose there is a decent person who is coldhearted and indifferent to the suffering and pain of others. Suppose also that he is very patient when he suffers. In addition, he also expects that other people should be just like him in difficult times. Such a person would not be the worst creature produced by nature. But even though he is not the sort of person who naturally loves and cares for others, he would still have in himself something far better than natural kindness. Would he not have a source of action which would give him a worth far greater than what comes from being good-natured and kind? Yes, without any doubt! Every person, whatever that person is like, can possess a moral worth which is, without any comparison, the greatest possible. In the case we have looked at, such a person can be loving and caring and generous towards others from duty, rather than because he wants by natural feeling to be that way.

Philosophical Fragments
Soren Kierkegaard

Suppose a king loved a poor and humble woman. This king was so much in love that his heart wasn't bothered by all the usual worries about love. He wasn't troubled by all the reasons the mind uses to convince the heart that love is impossible. And it was easy for him to do anything he wanted. All the foreign nations trembled because of his power. Each would certainly send ambassadors to congratulate him on his wedding. No lord or lady of his court would dare remind him that his wife had been so poor and humble. So let the harp be tuned. Let the poet's songs begin to be heard. Let there be a holiday while love celebrates its great victory. For love is glorious when it unites equals, but it is most triumphant when two people who were unequal are made equal through it.

Then there awakened in the king's heart an uneasy thought about their inequality. No one but a king who thinks kingly thoughts would have thought of it. And he spoke to no one about his worry. If he had, everyone would have said, "Your majesty, you are about to give a great favor to this humble woman. Her whole life is not long enough for her to be adequately grateful." This speech would have produced a great anger in the king. He would have commanded the execution of the speaker. This speech would have been high treason against the woman he loved. Yet by doing this he would have found, in still another way, the very thought which caused his grief.

So he struggled with his troubled thoughts alone. Would she be happy in her life at his side? Would she be able to be confident enough never to remember that he was a king and she had been a poor and humble woman? This was what the king wanted most of all for her to forget. For what if this memory were suddenly to stir in her soul? Just like a fantasy about another lover, this memory would draw her thoughts away from her husband. If she remembered that he was a king and she had been a humble woman, her thoughts would be lured away into the seclusion of a secret and private grief. Or if this memory occasionally and suddenly passed across her soul like death's shadow across a grave, where then would be the triumphant victory and glory of their love? Then she would have been happier if she had remained where she was. She would have been happily married and in her humble home. She would have been confident in her love and cheerful throughout the day.

What a great and rich abundance of grief is here laid bare. It is like ripened grain bent under the weight of its fruitfulness. It merely waits for the time of harvest when the king's thought will burst forth from this seed of sorrow. For even if the woman were willing to become as nothing, this couldn't satisfy the king. It wouldn't satisfy him precisely because he loves her and because it is harder for him to be the one who raised her up than to love her. And suppose she couldn't even understand what troubles him. For while we are talking in this way about human relations, we might even suppose their minds are so different that they couldn't understand one another on this matter. What a depth of grief sleeps in this unhappy love, and who dares to awaken it!

Our problem is now before us. And we invite the poet, unless he's already busy somewhere else, to address it. The poet's task will be to find a solution, some point of union, where love's understanding and triumph come about in truth, and the ruler's uneasiness is set to rest, and his sorrow banished. For the triumph of love is when two unequals are made equal. Yet, we must ask if it is even possible.

Tao Te Ching
Lao Tsu

A.

In this world we can see beautiful things, because other things are ugly. Because some things are not good, we can also know that there is good. What is and what is not always come about together. What is difficult and what isn't difficult complete each other. Long always contrasts with short. High is built upon low. Sound blends with voice. Front and back are never apart.

Therefore, the wise man does things by doing nothing, teaches without saying a word. Without any stop or pause, things come and go. The wise man makes them but doesn't hold on to them. The wise do things, but no one knows they did them. These things get done and then forgotten. That's why they last forever.

B.

If the gifted are not raised above everyone else, people will stop quarreling and fighting. If rare things aren't valued, no one will be a thief. If things people want aren't everywhere for them to see, their hearts won't be troubled.

So, here is how the wise rule. They fill people's stomachs and keep their hearts empty of desire. They weaken their people's ambitions but strengthen their bones. The wise keep people away from knowledge and desire. Then, the clever and crafty ones will be afraid to act. Doing things by doing nothing, everything will be fine.

C.

A good hiker leaves no tracks.
A good speaker makes no slip-ups.
A person who is good at counting doesn't need a calculator.
A well-made door can be locked without lock and key.
A well-tied rope needs no knot and yet can't be undone.

In the same way, a good man can take care of everyone. He doesn't need to reject anyone. He looks after all things and leaves nothing behind.

This is called "Following the Light."

A good man teaches the bad men.
Teaching the bad is how a good man learns.
If the teacher does not care for the bad,
And the student does not respect the good,
Everything will become confused, however clever they both are.

This is the most important part of the mystery.

D.

The sage does not have his own personal concerns.
He considers the concerns of others as his own.
I am good to those who are good. I am good to those who aren't good.
This is how goodness is brought about. I trust those who trust. I trust those who are suspicious. This is how trust is achieved.
The sage is withdrawn and unassuming.
People look where he looks and try to hear what he hears.
The sage considers all of them infants.

Treasure of the City of Ladies:
Advice to Princesses
Christine de Pisan

The two Holy lives are the active life and the contemplative life.
Here is what you must do if you wish to be saved. *The Bible*
tells of two paths which lead to Heaven, and it is impossible to enter
unless we follow one of these paths. One is called the contemplative
life, the other path is called the active life. But what are the life of
contemplation and the life of action?

The contemplative life is a way of serving God in which a
person so fully desires Our Lord that she completely forgets everyone
else. In order to achieve a very great and burning concentration on
her Creator, she no longer remembers father, mother, children, or
even herself. She constantly thinks of Him and Him alone. Everything
else is nothing to her. She doesn't experience poverty. She pays no
attention to the troubles and torments which burden other people.
She scorns everything that is of the world, especially its pleasures.
She keeps herself alone, apart from all human society. Her knees are
bent, her hands joined together, her heart raised by high thoughts,
her eyes look to Heaven. The perfect contemplative is often in such
ecstasy that she doesn't seem to be herself.

The comfort, peace, and joy she feels can't be described, for
she is tasting the glories and joys of Paradise. She sees God in spirit
through thought. She burns in her love and is perfectly content in
this world. God gives her pure and holy thoughts which come from
Heaven. There is no other joy like it. But I regret that I can only talk
about it indirectly, as a blind person might talk about colors. It has
been made clear that this life is more agreeable to God than any
other. Of this holy and exalted life I am not worthy to speak or
describe it as it deserves.

The active life is another way of serving God. In the active life,
a person will be so charitable that, if she could, she would give
service to everyone for the love of God. She goes to hospitals, visits
the poor and the sick, and helps them at her own expense and effort
for the love of God. She has great pity for people she sees in sin or
misery. She weeps for them as though their troubles and distress

were her own. She is always striving to do good. Her heart burns with the desire to do works of mercy. Such a woman bears all injuries and troubles patiently for the love of God.

The active life has more use in the world than the other one. They are both great and excellent. But Our Lord Jesus Christ Himself judged which is the greater. Mary Magdalene, who represents the contemplative life, was seated at the foot of our Lord. She had no thought for anything else and burned with her holy love. And Mary Martha, by whom the active life is understood, was the hostess of Our Lord. She worked in the house serving Jesus and the Apostles and complained that Mary, her sister, didn't help her. But Our Lord excused her. He said, "Martha, you are very diligent. Your work is good and needed. But Mary has chosen the better part." By this "part" which she has chosen, can be understood which life is greater. Although the active life is of great excellence and necessary for the help of many, contemplation—which is to give up the world and all its cares to think only of Him—is the greatest and worthiest perfection.

The good princess says to herself: "I must decide which of these paths I wish to take. But first I ought to think of my strengths and weaknesses. If I consider these things honestly, I find that although I have some good intentions, I am too weak to avoid all pleasures and to suffer great pain. And my spirit is weak through indecision. Since I feel myself to be this way, I should not imagine that I am better than I am." Though God says, "You must give up father and mother for my sake," yet I know that I wouldn't be able to fulfill my pledge. I couldn't leave husband, children, everyday life, and all worldly concerns. I shouldn't try to do something I couldn't do. So I could not lead the life of contemplation. What shall I do then? Should I choose the active life? But how could I ever manage to give up my position of power in the world? Although I know very well that there is nothing else I have and desire except You and know that all other pleasure is nothing, I still don't have the strength in myself to abandon every worldly thing. I am very frightened about what to do. Since I see very well that I am not the sort of person who can entirely choose either life, I will therefore try hard to find something in the middle. St. Paul, himself, gives the same advice: "So I will take as much as I can from both lives according to my ability."

Self-Reliance
Ralph Waldo Emerson

There comes a time in every man's education when he comes to the conclusion that envying other people is a kind of ignorance, and that imitating other people is a kind of suicide. He discovers that he must take himself, for better or worse, as he is. He discovers that, though the universe is full of good things, none of them can nourish him. He is nourished only through his own labour or through the gifts nature has given to him. The power which lives in every person is new in nature, and no one except the individual knows what he can do. Even he doesn't know until he has tried.

It isn't for nothing that a certain face or a certain fact makes an impression on him and on no one else. His eye has viewed the scene so that the particular person's face and the particular fact might be seen and revealed through him to others. Usually we only half express ourselves. It is as if we were ashamed of the divine idea which each of us represents. This divine idea in each of us can be trusted as long as we are faithful to it. But God does not want His work done by cowards. A man is happy and relieved when he has put his heart into his work and done his best. But if he has not done this, all that he has said and his inspiration will desert him; he will invent nothing; he will lose hope.

Trust yourself! Every heart is tuned to that string. Accept the place that God has found for you and the friends you have. Great men have always done so and have trusted, like children, in the circumstances of their lives. They showed that what could most be counted on was already in their hearts and would come out in the work of their minds and hands. *We* are now these men and must accept the same destiny. We are neither children nor sick people living in a protected corner. We are not cowards trying to escape a revolution. We are guides and benefactors, obeying God and fighting against darkness and evil.

"We Cannot Live for Ourselves Alone"
Vernon E. Jordan, Jr.

Few observers have penetrated so deeply into the inner workings of American society than Alexis de Tocqueville. Even today, 146 years after the publication of his *Democracy in America*, most of his insights retain a relevance for contemporary society. And among them is the following profound comment:

> Among the laws that rule human societies there is one which seems to be more precise and clear than all others. If men are to remain civilized or to become more so, the art of associating together must grow and improve in the same ratio in which the equality of conditions is increased.

This brief quote contains two themes that are very important to de Tocqueville's view of America: the tendency to form voluntary associations to order our lives and the democratic desire for equality. And de Tocqueville wisely links the two; indeed, he makes them inseparable. In so doing, he provides us with a framework in which to place our voluntary efforts to improve our communities.

For just as no man is an island, separate and apart from others, so too, no community can see itself in isolation from other towns and cities, from the nation as a whole, or from countries and people far from our borders. In our times especially, we have seen how racial and economic problems penetrate even the most self-contained rich communities. We have seen the problems of rural poverty and racism become the core problems of our urban crises. Now we see them becoming part of suburban life as well.

There is no hiding place in the modern world. There can be no isolation from social problems. If our society is to grow and prosper, if our civilization is to flourish, then indeed our voluntary agencies must be directed to ensuring the equality toward which we have strived.

This is not to de-emphasize the proper role of government. Because government has great resources, legal powers of persuasion, and is politically accountable, it must hold a central position in organizing our society's efforts toward political, social, and economic equality.

But, as de Tocqueville pointed out, the danger that faces democratic governments is the passivity of the people: the tendency for individuals not to take personal responsibility for *social* actions. Because voluntary associations provide the opportunity for personal involvement, they become the cement that holds our society together.

True self-interest has to do not only with looking out for yourself, but also with the preservation of society's goals and values, and with the creation of conditions in which all people may get ahead and share in the responsibilities of citizenship. Neglect of this true self-interest leads, as we have seen, to racial conflict, to poverty and the bitterness that comes with poverty, and to the breakdown of rules of conduct and civilized behavior.

What is so often called the urban crises or the racial crises is often nothing more than the result of people confusing selfishness with true self-interest.

It is clear to me that the spirit of true self-interest and of volunteer work as a means of changing our society are very important to our nation's future. And linked to this concept of creative volunteerism is the need to encourage voluntary activity among all people, and not to restrict participation in volunteer work to those with time and money.

One way to encourage greater participation in volunteer work is to increase the incentives for charitable giving. In its efforts to simplify the tax code, the government has accidentally discouraged low and moderate income families from giving. In changing the standard tax deduction, the government has removed the tax savings from seven out of ten taxpayers—mostly lower income—who do not itemize deductions. This shifts support for charities to the small number of better-off Americans who receive tax rewards for their giving—rewards denied other Americans.

There are two dangers here—charitable giving may become an elitist function, and many millions of Americans may not be encouraged to participate at the simplest level of charitable giving.

To state the problem is to suggest the solution: Tax laws should be changed so that people who take the standard deduction can also take charitable deductions.

A second way of encouraging volunteerism is to show people that in addition to charitable giving, it also includes working to correct injustices, that is, advocacy.

Most people think that volunteerism means providing money and services to people who need them. In doing this, which deals with the causes that create the demand for those services, advocacy has been neglected.

We often consider it the proper role of voluntary activity to provide assistance to those in poor health and in poor living conditions. We don't as often think about advocating public policy changes in our national health system, in slum rehabilitation public housing, and discrimination in housing. And yet without dealing positively with these larger issues, volunteerism forces itself into the position of handing out band-aids for a sick society.

At the center of a positive response must be the understanding that we are all linked together in such a way that in our efforts to help others, we make our own lives more satisfying and more secure.

Unit IV

Reflections on Politics and Community Service

Leviathan
Thomas Hobbes

Nature has made man roughly equal in body and mind. When everything is considered, the difference between one man and another is not very great. The case of bodily strength serves as a good example. The weakest man has enough strength to kill the strongest. He can do this either by some trick or by using a weapon or by joining with other men. The same is true of men's minds. Inequalities can be made up by various means.

This rough equality in ability produces in every man the equal hope of getting what he wants. So when two men desire something which only one man can have, this equality encourages both to strive for it. They therefore become enemies. Each man tries to destroy or defeat the other in order to get what he needs to keep alive or to enjoy his life. If we consider what men are like when they do not live in societies, we find that they become enemies. When one defeats the other, the victor must, in turn, expect a third person to try to take away what he has won.

So it is clear what men are like when there is no outside power to keep them all in fear. Such a state of nature becomes a condition of war. In such a war every man struggles with every other man. War does not only mean constant fighting. A period of time during which there is a willingness to fight, and fighting is commonly known and accepted, is also called war. So in the state of nature, every man is every other man's enemy. There is no safety or security except one's own strength and trickery. In this state of things there can be no factories or stores, because products are always unsafe. There can be no farming, no trading, no large buildings, no arts, no sciences, no society. Worst of all there would be continual fear and danger of violent death. The life of man would be solitary, poor, nasty, brutish, and short.

This state of nature might not actually have existed, and I certainly do not believe it existed throughout the world. Yet if we look at what men are now like in societies we can convince ourselves how men would be in a purely natural condition. At night we all lock our houses, and when we walk the streets we are constantly on guard. This shows that we believe that only fear of an outside power keeps men in check. Nations and kings who have nothing to fear act toward one another just as we described individual men acting in a state of nature. When a peaceful society falls into civil war we see what men are really like outside of society.

The Confessions
St. Augustine of Hippo

God, your law punishes theft. This law is written in our hearts, and no amount of evil or crime can erase it. We can see this because no thief, not even a rich one, will let another man, even one who is very poor, steal from him. Yet, I both wanted to steal and did steal. And what is so surprising is that I was not forced to do it by any need. I stole something which I already had. I stole pears, though I already had pears which were much better than the ones I took. I had no wish to eat what I stole. What I enjoyed was stealing itself.

Near my parents' garden was a neighbor's pear tree. Though it was loaded with fruit, the pears looked rotten. I and some friends got the idea of shaking the pears off the tree and carrying them away. We set out late at night and stole all the fruit we could carry. We tasted a few and then threw the rest to the pigs. The pleasure we felt was simply in doing something which was forbidden. We took no pleasure in eating the pears, nor in being out late at night.

The Republic
Plato

Do people behave justly because they want to? Or are they just and fair because they are afraid to be unjust? To answer these questions, let us pretend we can give both the just and unjust man the freedom and power to do whatever they please. Then in our imaginations we can see where their desires will lead them. The just person will be no different from the unjust person. For he looks to his self-interest just as much as the unjust man does. Only fear of the law makes him just. Let me tell you a story about a man who had such freedom.

People say that he was a shepherd in the service of the king of Lydia. After a great rainstorm and an earthquake, the ground opened up where he was caring for sheep, and he went into the opening in the earth. The story goes on to say that he saw many marvels there, among which was a hollow bronze horse with little doors. When he peeped in, he saw the body of a giant with a gold ring on its hand. He took the ring and left.

When the shepherds held their monthly meeting to report to the king about his flocks, he also attended, wearing the ring. While he was sitting there twisting the ring on his finger, he happened to turn it so that the stone faced his palm. When he did this, the story goes on, he became invisible to those who sat around him. They spoke about him as if he were not there. He was amazed and fumbled with his ring. When he turned the stone out, he became visible again. He tested this many times and found that the ring really possessed this power of making him invisible when he wanted. So with the help of this ring, he seduced the king's wife and got her to help him kill the king and take over his kingdom.

Now suppose we have two such rings. Let's give one to a just man and the other to an unjust man. It is hard to believe that even a just man would stop himself from stealing if he knew he would never get caught.

The Peloponnesian Wars
Thucydides

Athens and Sparta, the two most powerful cities in Greece, had been at war with one another for many years. Athens, a great naval power, controlled most of the islands in the Aegean Sea. It was creating an empire, but some of the islands were not eager to join. One such island was Melos, which had been colonized by Sparta and wished to remain neutral. In the sixteenth year of the war, an Athenian fleet sailed to the island of Melos. As soon as the Athenian army landed, they sent ambassadors to negotiate with the most important men on the island.

Athenians: We don't plan to pretend we have a right to be on your island. In return, don't you bother telling us you won't join our enemies, the Spartans, or that you've never hurt us. All these claims would only hide the real issue. We both know the way the world is. Right and wrong come into play only between people whose power is equal. Otherwise the strong do what they can. The weak suffer whatever is necessary.

Melians: You tell us to forget what is right and only consider what is in our self-interest. Agreed! Even so, it couldn't be useful to anyone—us or you—to deny us a privilege always allowed those in great danger. When someone is threatened, he is permitted to bring up what is fair and right. At those times, one is even allowed to use arguments which aren't quite logical if he can get them accepted. You Athenians should want to protect this custom too. You'll need it if you're ever defeated. For people will avenge themselves on you.

Athenians: We're not afraid of the end of our empire. It is worse to have subjects who attack and overpower their rulers. We're here, therefore, for the present interests of our empire. We want to rule you for the good of us both.

Melians: We'd love to hear how it's as good for us to serve you as for you to rule us.

Athenians: You would gain by not being destroyed. We would gain by not destroying you.

Melians: So we can't be neutral?

Athenians: No. Your hostility can't hurt us much. But to our subjects, your neutrality may look like our weakness.

Melians: But we're not in the same category as your subjects. They are either your colonists or those who have rebelled against you. We're neither.

Athenians: To our subjects, there are only two kinds of people. There are those we rule and those we don't rule. And our subjects believe if we don't rule a people, it is because they're strong. If we don't attack them, it is because we are afraid. You're weaker than many of our subjects. We can't let you escape the masters of the sea.

Melians: All right. You won't let us talk about justice. We'll talk about self-interest. Our interests and yours are the same. Many cities and islands are still neutral. If you attack us, they'll think they're next. So they'll become your enemies even though they wouldn't have thought of doing so.

Athenians: Neutrals on land don't concern us. It's the islanders like you and our discontented subjects who worry us. Both could take rash steps and lead themselves and us into danger.

Melians: If your subjects will risk so much to be free of you, how can you expect us to submit to you? We're still free. Shouldn't we try everything to avoid losing that?

Athenians: If honor and shame were at stake, then perhaps you should. But they're not at issue because we're so much stronger than you. All you have to worry about is simply how to preserve yourselves.

Melians: Anything can happen in war. Numbers aren't always the crucial thing. If we give up, we have no hope. If we fight, there's still a chance.

Athenians: Hope is very dangerous. Only those who have something to spare, something extra, can afford to hope. Hope can tempt us to absurd actions. We only recognize how flimsy our hope is when we are ruined. You are weak. Your survival hangs on a single throw of the dice. You can't risk hope. That's the way to destruction.

Melians: We know you are stronger. But we trust in the help of the gods since we are just men fighting against unjust men.

Athenians: We have gods too. And there is a law that gods and men rule wherever they can. We didn't create this law. It was here before us. It will still exist after us. We act by it knowing that you, having our power, would do the same.

The Melians and Athenians then went to war. After a hard fight, Athens won. The Athenians killed all the Melian men. They sold the women and children into slavery.

The Iliad
Homer

In the tenth year of the war between the Greeks and the Trojans, the greatest Greek warrior, Achilles, killed the most courageous and strongest Trojan, Hector. Because Hector had killed Achilles' closest friend, the Greek was not satisfied by his enemy's death. For days, Achilles insulted Hector's dead body as the Trojan's father, King Priam, longing to recover his son's body for burial, remained helpless in his city. Each day, Achilles dragged Hector's dead body through the dust. At night he returned to his tent to rest, refusing to eat. This day was no different. He rested in his tent, waiting for the dawn when he would continue his revenge against the dead man.

Suddenly, Achilles saw a tall, kingly, old man before him. It was Priam, king of the Trojans, and father of Hector. Priam kneeled before the Greek and kissed the hands which had killed so many of his sons. "Achilles, remember your own father," Priam said. "He must be my age. Perhaps right now in a faraway country, people are causing him pain. But nothing he suffers can compare with my misery. He is happy knowing that you, his son, are still alive. I once had fifty sons, but now most are dead. Yet worst of all is the death of my best son, Hector. You killed him, and now I come all alone into your camp to ask for his body. Take pity on me. Remember your own father. For I am to be pitied more than any man alive. What other man has had to come through great danger to kiss the hand of his son's killer?"

Priam's words stirred in Achilles a great sadness for his own father. He pushed the old man's hands away gently. Priam sat on the floor. Achilles remained on the stool. They sat near one another, each remembering those who were not there. Priam wept for his dead son, Hector. Achilles, looking at Priam's face, wept for his own absent father and for his dead friend. The young warrior and the old king wept together.

When the Greek had enough of his grief, he got up from his chair. He took the old king's hand and raised him to his feet. "How could you have risked coming to my ships, old man? Your heart must be iron. Sit on this chair, and you and I will end our grief.

What's the use of weeping? We both know what everyone's life is like. The gods have two jars. One holds good things, the other holds troubles and misery. Each person gets some of both. Sometimes one has good fortune. Other times one has bad fortune. This is how it was for my own father. He was a ruler of men, had riches and property, and was given a goddess for a wife. Yet, he too received evil. Unlike you, he had only one son, and I give him no help as he grows old. I sit here, far away, bringing pain and sorrow to you and your children. And you, Priam, once ruled this whole area with your sons. Now your kingdom must fight constantly, and your sons are dead. Don't mourn endlessly. You can never bring Hector back to life."

"Achilles," said the old king, "don't make me sit here while my dead son still lies in the dust. Please let me see him and take him home. The presents I've brought are valuable. Take them and give me my son."

Achilles frowned and stared at Priam. "Don't stir me up, old man! I give him back because I give him back. Don't remind me of my own grief, or I may strike you even here in my tent."

Priam was frightened. The young Greek warrior, moving like a lion, left the tent. He took the ransom out of Priam's wagon and then went to find serving-maids. He ordered them to wash Hector's dead body. He did this because he was afraid Priam would break down at the sight of his son's dirty, broken body. The old man might be unable to hold back his anger. Achilles was afraid that this would remind him of his own grief, and he would, there in his tent, kill the old man.

Achilles returned to his tent and spoke. "Priam, we must both eat. Even Niobe, whose twelve children were killed, ate when she was worn out with crying. Afterwards, you can take your son home to bury him."

The two men ate. These two men, who had wept and mourned together, now looked at one another. Each admired the other. Achilles appeared as a god to the old king. Priam appeared brave and dignified to the young warrior. The two men then slept. At dawn, Priam put his son on the wagon and took him home to bury him and to prepare his people to fight again.

The Prince
Niccolo Machiavelli

I wish now to speak about how a ruler should treat his friends and subjects. Many famous authors have written about this, and I am afraid you will think that I am being arrogant for writing about it again. This is especially so since what I have to say is so different from what the famous authors of the past have said. They have written about imaginary governments which don't exist in reality. To me it seems more useful to write down the simple truth of the matter. There is such a great difference between how human beings actually live, and how they ought to live. A ruler who ignores what is being done by human beings in order to think about what ought to be done will bring about his own destruction. Since a ruler always has subjects who are not good, he too must learn how not to be good.

Let us therefore stop talking about imaginary things and start saying what is true about a ruler. All men, rulers included, are said to have qualities for which they are praised and blamed. Some men are called generous, others stingy, some cruel, others merciful, some treacherous, others faithful, some cowardly, others brave, some religious, others unreligious, and so on. Everyone will agree that it would be nice if a ruler had all the qualities mentioned above that are considered good. However, it is impossible to have them all, for human nature is not like that. The ruler should be smart enough not to get the reputation for having those bad qualities which could cause him to lose power. As for the other bad qualities, he should not worry too much about his reputation. If he thinks about the matter carefully he will see that if he tries to acquire certain qualities which seem good, he might lose his power. On the other hand, some other qualities which seem bad will help him to increase his power.

The Labor Question
Frederick Douglass

This title, "The Labor Question," will sound vague and indefinite to conservatives who are uneasy when they think about great issues. Logicians may also rightly complain of this indefiniteness, if they don't look deeply into the question. Like all great social movements, the labor movement has both good and evil in it. We must look at both honestly. Whenever human beings try to change their way of life from something familiar to something better but only vaguely understood, the change always carries a mixture of good and evil. Evil, or what seems to us to be evil, is a necessary part of progress. It is a law of existence and accompanies all movement and change.

In this country, the first great step which was taken to free the working man was the abolition of slavery, the abolition of the right to own another human being. Unfortunately, many of those most active in the anti-slavery movement have no higher motive than improving their own conditions of life. They are not concerned about other people, and they don't think about the conditions of life. The real object of all who want to free human beings from unfairness must be to understand the ways in which the products of human labor are distributed in society. We all know that at the present time this distribution is unfair.

Those who don't engage in production get a larger share of things than do those who actually do the work. The result of this is the discontent of laborers. This discontent increases as working people become better educated and aware of what is going on around them. The worker of today is not satisfied with the things which satisfied his parents. This is true both of immigrants from China and Europe as well as freed slaves.

Certain decent but conservative people are shocked at the evidence of widespread discontent among working people. These good people are blind to the fact that although their own conditions of life have improved greatly, the conditions of life of working people have not improved at all. Working people desire to improve their conditions of life very much, even if they can't describe their desires very well or act on them very wisely. One fact must be understood and admitted. In all societies which have been governed by the high pressure principle of competition—the principle of "every man for himself"—poverty has become a fixed part of that society and is on the increase.

The central question before us is whether civilization has been designed primarily for the preservation of Property or for the preservation of Man. Decent people can only give one answer, although they may differ on the ways of achieving this goal. The happiness of human beings must be the chief goal of any society which deserves to exist. Any society which has increased dramatically its power to produce goods and yet keeps seventy percent of its citizens from enjoying these goods, has not realized the fundamental goal of society. Such a society is a failure. Yet even in America, any worker who didn't earn a salary for a month would be reduced to asking for charity. It is this anxiety more than actual poverty which makes the discontent among American working people so strong. It is ignorance of remedies that makes this discontent so dangerous.

The labor movement is a fundamental human concern, and it is growing rapidly. It will make itself heard by the very force of numbers if by nothing else. It is the duty of those who have already benefited from the labor movement to work for it. They must seek, honestly and fairly, remedies for this discontent. They must be careful to try to preserve what is good in present social and economic conditions, while destroying what is bad. No movement which involves such large numbers can be safely ignored. It must be treated fairly, or society will be torn apart. The demands which people make together are always just. Even if ignorance and prejudice make these demands seem unreasonable, the guiding impulse is one that seeks to right some wrong.

The German Ideology
Karl Marx

In every age, the members of the ruling class have the same ideas. These ideas rule the whole society. That is, the class which owns the property, factories, and all the means of material production, at the same time controls the means of mental production. The ruling ideas of a society are the same ideas of the ruling class. These ideas express and justify the power of the ruling class over the rest of society.

Just as there is division of labor in factories, there is also division of labor in the field of thought. Some members of the ruling class earn their living by being the thinkers of that class. They come up with the ideas which express what the ruling class wants to think about itself. Other members of the ruling class don't have time to make up these ideas. They are busy putting these ideas into practice. Sometimes it seems that the thinkers of the ruling class come into conflict with the doers. But, in reality, this conflict never comes to anything because, ultimately, the members of the ruling class all have the same beliefs.

It is easy to be wrong about this. It is easy to imagine that ideas have an existence which is independent of the ruling class, the class which controls money and the means of producing the necessities of life. Historians often make this mistake. They think that ideas are the important causes of social arrangements. They think, for example, that because the ideas of honor and loyalty were dominant in one society, the ruling class was therefore composed of aristocrats. And, that because the ideas of freedom and equality were dominant in another society, therefore the middle class ruled. The ruling classes themselves think this. They also think that the ideas of their class are eternal and therefore true. They think that they act as they do because they believe these ideas to be true.

However, it is important to keep the following in mind when trying to understand what is important in history. Ruling classes don't last forever. They are, sooner or later, overthrown by one of the classes of people they rule. For example, during the French Revolution, the king and aristocrats were overthrown in a revolution begun by the middle class. Whenever a class of people overthrows the ruling class and puts itself in the other's place, it has to persuade many people that the things and ideas which concern them also concern everyone else. For example the middle class has to persuade the working class that its interest will also be served by following the middle class in the revolution. The class which is starting the revolution has to give its ideas the appearance of being independent of the interests of that class. It must persuade itself and the other classes that its ideas are eternal and true.

It can do this because, in the beginning, it can claim to be the representative of all the non-ruling classes against the ruling class. Its ideas represent the complaints of other members of society against the ruling class. It can, also, actually help people from other classes. However, it does this by making them similar to itself both in the way it lives and thinks. When the middle class overthrew the king and aristocracy in the French Revolution, many members of the working class were indeed able to better themselves. However, they could only better themselves by becoming members of the middle class in their ideas and hopes. This is because the middle class had all the money and owned the means of producing the necessities of life. If a person wanted to better his life, there was nothing else he could do but become in all ways a member of the middle class.

But those whose lives have not been improved are not fooled. They know that the ideas of the ruling class only express and justify the power of this class over the rest of society. Because of this, these people know the truths of history better than the historians do. They are not deceived as the historians are, by being members of the ruling class.

The Summa Theologica
St. Thomas Aquinas

Laws made by man are either just or unjust. If they are just, they rule our conscience because just laws are derived from the eternal law of God. As it says in Proverbs in the Bible, "By Me, kings rule and lawgivers decree just things." Laws are considered just on account of the purpose they serve, the authority of the lawgiver, and their form. They are just when the purpose is the common good, when the lawgiver does not exceed his right to make certain kinds of laws, and when the form of the laws places burdens on the subjects proportionate to their position in society. This last condition is true since each man is a part of the community; each, in all that he is and has, belongs to the community. This is no different from the way in which any part, in all that exists, belongs to the whole. There we see that nature often imposes a greater burden on one part for the sake of the whole. For the very same reason, there are sometimes laws which do not impose equal but rather proportionate burdens, and these are just and legal laws which bind our consciences.

On the other hand, laws may be unjust in two ways. First, a law may be contrary to human good through being opposed to the things we have just mentioned. In respect to the goal or purpose, an authority might impose burdensome laws on its subjects, which are not for the common good but rather the ruler's own selfish ends. Or a ruler might make a law which goes beyond the power committed to him. Or a law in its form may look toward the common good but not impose burdens which have a due proportion to the positions of the subjects within the community. All these are acts of violence rather than laws. As St. Augustine says, "A law that is not just does not seem to be a law at all." Therefore, these laws do not bind in conscience at all, except possibly to avoid scandal or disturbance. To avoid scandal and disturbance, a man should even yield his right. For according to Matthew, "If a man takes away your shirt, give him your cloak also; and whoever forces you to go one mile, go the second with him."

Secondly, laws can be unjust through being opposed to the divine good. Such would be laws by tyrants forcing idolatry or anything else contrary to the divine law. Laws of this sort must never be followed. As is stated in the Acts of the Apostles, "We ought to obey God rather than men."

There are a number of objections which could be made to what has just been said.

The first objection is that a human law never binds a man's conscience because an inferior power cannot impose its law on the judgment of a higher power. But the power of man, which makes human law, is beneath divine power. Therefore human law cannot impose itself on the judgment of our consciences, which is based on divine law. To this I reply: the Apostle Paul says in the Epistle to the Romans that all human power is from God. "Therefore he who resists the power" in matters that are within its scope "resists the commands of God." So, such a person becomes guilty in his conscience.

The second objection is the following: the judgment made by our conscience depends primarily on the commandments of God. But sometimes the commandments of God are made void by human laws. As Matthew says, "You have made God's laws null and void out of respect for your tradition." Therefore, human law does not bind our consciences. I reply that this argument is true of laws which are contrary to God's commandments, for these commandments are beyond the scope of human power. In such matters, human law should not be obeyed.

There is also a third objection. Human laws often bring to men both injury and a loss of character. For according to Isaiah, "Shame on you who make unjust laws and burdensome decrees. You deprive the poor of justice and rob the weakest of my people of their rights." Since it is lawful for all to avoid oppression and violence, therefore human laws do not bind our conscience. I reply that this argument is true of any law that imposes an unjust burden on its subjects. The power that man holds from God does not extend to this. So, in such matters, a man is not bound to obey the law, provided he can avoid causing scandal or inflicting an even worse injury by his disobedience.

When considering these matters another question arises. Should a human law be changed whenever a better law comes along? I answer that human law is rightly changed when such a change helps attain the common good. But, to a certain extent, the change of any law, even an unjust law, harms the common good. This is because custom helps a great deal in getting us to observe all laws. We can see this by noticing that anything that is done contrary to our usual customs, even in small matters, is looked at as a serious offense. So when any law is changed, the power of law itself is diminished insofar as a custom is abolished. Therefore, human law should never be changed, unless, in some way or other, the common good is compensated according to the extent of the harm done by breaking our habit of obeying laws. Such compensation occurs either from the very great and obvious benefit conferred by the new law or from the extreme urgency of the case, because the existing law is clearly unjust or because its observance causes great harm. As the great legal thinker Gratian says, "In making a new law, one must have evidence of the benefits which will be derived before changing a law which has, for a long time, been considered just."

Letter from Birmingham Jail
Martin Luther King, Jr.

You will express a great deal of anxiety over our willingness to break laws. This is certainly a legitimate concern. Since we so diligently urge people to obey the Supreme Court's decision of 1954 outlawing segregation in the public schools, at first glance it may seem rather paradoxical for us consciously to break laws. One may well ask: "How can you advocate breaking some laws and obeying others?" The answer lies in the fact that there are two types of laws: just and unjust. I would be the first to advocate obeying just laws. One has not only a legal but a moral responsibility to obey just laws. Conversely, one has a moral responsibility to disobey unjust laws. I would agree with St. Augustine that "an unjust law is no law at all."

Now, what is the difference between the two? How does one determine whether a law is just or unjust? A just law is a manmade code that squares with the moral law or the law of God. An unjust law is a code that is out of harmony with the moral law. To put it in the terms of St. Thomas Aquinas: An unjust law is a human law that is not rooted in eternal law and natural law. Any law that uplifts human personality is just. Any law that degrades human personality is unjust.

All segregation statutes are unjust because segregation distorts the soul and damages the personality. It gives the segregator a false sense of superiority, and the segregated a false sense of inferiority. Segregation, to use the terminology of the Jewish philosopher Martin Buber, substitutes an "I-it" relationship for an "I-thou" relationship, and ends up relegating persons to the status of things. Hence segregation is not only politically, economically, and sociologically unsound, it is morally wrong and sinful. Paul Tillich has said that sin is separation. Is not segregation an existential expression of man's tragic separation, his awful estrangement, his terrible sinfulness? Thus it is that I can urge men to obey the 1954 decision of the Supreme Court, for it is morally right, and I can urge them to disobey segregation ordinances, for they are morally wrong.

Let us consider a more concrete example of just and unjust laws. An unjust law is a code that a numerical or power majority group compels a minority group to obey but does not make binding on itself. This is difference made legal. By the same token, a just law is a code that a majority compels a minority to follow and that it is willing to follow itself. This is sameness made legal.

Let me give another explanation. A law is unjust if it is inflicted on a minority that, as a result of being denied the right to vote, had no part in enacting or devising the law. Who can say that the legislature of Alabama which set up that state's segregation laws was democratically elected? Throughout Alabama all sorts of devious methods are used to prevent Negroes from becoming registered voters, and there are some counties in which, even though Negroes constitute a majority of the population, not a single Negro is registered. Can any law enacted under such circumstances be considered democratically structured?

Sometimes a law is just on its face and unjust in its application. For instance, I have been arrested on a charge of parading without a permit. Now, there is nothing wrong in having an ordinance which requires a permit for a parade. But such an ordinance becomes unjust when it is used to maintain segregation and to deny citizens the First Amendment privilege of peaceful assembly and protest.

I hope you are able to see the distinction I am trying to point out. In no sense do I advocate evading or defying the law, as would the rabid segregationist. That would lead to anarchy. One who breaks an unjust law must do so openly, lovingly, and with a willingness to accept the penalty. I submit that an individual who breaks a law that conscience tells him is unjust, and who willingly accepts the penalty of imprisonment in order to arouse the conscience of the community over its injustice, is in reality expressing the highest respect for law.

Of course, there is nothing new about this kind of civil disobedience. It was evidenced sublimely in the refusal of Shadrach, Meshach, and Abednego to obey the laws of Nebuchadnezzar, on the ground that a higher moral law was at stake. It was practiced superbly by the early Christians, who were willing to face hungry lions and the excruciating pain of chopping blocks rather than submit to certain unjust laws of the Roman Empire. To a degree, academic freedom is a reality today because Socrates practiced civil disobedience. In our own nation, the Boston Tea Party represented a massive act of civil disobedience.

We should never forget that everything Adolf Hitler did in Germany was "legal," and everything the Hungarian freedom fighters did in Hungary was "illegal." It was "illegal" to aid and comfort a Jew in Hitler's Germany. Even so, I am sure that, had I lived in Germany at the time, I would have aided and comforted my Jewish brothers. If today I lived in a Communist country where certain principles dear to the Christian faith are suppressed, I would openly advocate disobeying that country's antireligious laws.

Unit V

Reflections on Tutoring and Working with Children

The Apology
Plato

Meletus has accused Socrates of corrupting the young people in Athens. He has taken him to court, and it is here that Socrates is defending himself.

Socrates: Meletus, you think it's very important for young people to be exposed to the best possible influences, don't you?

Meletus: Of course.

Socrates: Very well, then tell the court who it is that has the best influence on the young.

Meletus: The laws.

Socrates: Do you mean that they can educate young people and make them better?

Meletus: Yes, I do.

Socrates: How about all the spectators in this court? Are they also able to educate young people and make them better?

Meletus: Yes, they are.

Socrates: Then Meletus, according to you, everybody in Athens has a good influence on the young—everybody except me. Is that what you mean?

Meletus: Socrates, that is exactly what I mean.

Socrates: Meletus, you have just shown that you have absolutely no interest in the education of young people. You're pretending to be interested only because you're out to get me. Let me show you how I know. Do you think that everybody in this court is a good horse trainer? Of course you don't. Most people in this court would harm horses if they tried to train them. You know that horse training is very difficult. Is educating young people any less difficult? Not very many people know how to do it.

We Athenians would be very lucky if you were right. If only it were true that only one person had a bad influence on young people and everyone else had a good influence. But we both know this isn't true. This is how I know you are not interested in young people at all but are only out to get me.

But let's go on to something else. Is it better to live in a good community or in a bad one? In other words, is there anyone who would rather be harmed by his fellow citizens than benefited by them? Answer me like a good fellow; the law says you must.

Meletus: Of course not.

Socrates: Well then, when you accuse me of trying to harm young people, do you mean that I do it on purpose or accidentally?

Meletus: On purpose.

Socrates: Are you so much smarter than I am Meletus? We have just agreed that it is better to live in a good community than in a bad one. Yet now you say that I am harming young people and thus making Athens worse. If you thought about it for even one minute you would see that no one would harm young people on purpose. He would only be harming himself. If I ever did harm young people, I did it accidentally. It was because I failed as a teacher. If this is true you should have taken me aside and tried to persuade me to change. But you never did that. You never spoke to me until you got me in court. Now you want to punish me, not to teach me. This is how I know that you are not at all interested either in education or in young people.

The Republic
Plato

Socrates is speaking with his young friend, Glaucon.

Socrates: Glaucon, let's try to think about what human life is like ordinarily, and what it might be like for someone who somehow got to know the truth about it. Imagine that all human beings live in a cave under the earth. The cave has an entrance open to the light of day. But the human beings are chained so that they can neither move, nor turn toward the opening, nor even turn toward each other. They have been chained in this way since their childhood. Imagine also that there is a fire burning and glowing within the cave. It is above and behind the prisoners, casting shadows on the wall in front of them. They cannot see the fire. All the prisoners can see are shadows of themselves and of each other on the wall. They also see shadows cast by anything that is carried behind their backs between the glowing fire and themselves.

Glaucon: This is a strange image, Socrates, and the prisoners are strange prisoners.

Socrates: In many ways, these prisoners are just like us. Do you think these people will see anything of themselves or of each other except the shadows cast on the wall?

Glaucon: No, not if they are not able to look in any direction except straight ahead.

Socrates: And what about the things carried past them, behind their backs? Would they see those things themselves or only their shadows? Even worse, could they even know if they were missing something?

Glaucon: No, perhaps they could not tell the difference.

Socrates: Would their conversations with each other be about anything real? Wouldn't they think that the shadows were real things?

Glaucon: Yes, of course.

Socrates: Could these people ever be freed and healed of their ignorance?

Glaucon: I don't know.

Socrates: What if something like this happened? I'm not sure how it would happen. Suppose one prisoner was freed from his chains and forced suddenly to stand up, to turn around, to look, and to try to walk. Wouldn't he be confused and frightened when he saw the glow of the fire, and when he saw the objects which cast the shadows he had been looking at before? But, what if he were forced to go on? Suppose he were dragged out into the light of day. Wouldn't he be frightened and confused again, as he saw the things that exist in the light of day, in the light of the sun? All he had seen before were shadows of things by firelight. Now he has to look upon things in the sun. At first, he couldn't look directly at these things, but he could look at their shadows and at their reflections in ponds. After a while, he could look directly at the things in the light of the sun. Finally, after much difficulty, he would be able to look with gladness upon the sun itself.

How might the person who had gone through this journey think about where he had been before and where he was now? I guess that the first part of his life might not seem so important anymore. His recent discoveries might seem like the most important things in the world. Also, after he thought about it, he might suspect that his fellow prisoners would not be glad to see him again, especially if they thought he knew something they didn't. They would especially resent him if he told them that the things they have spent their lives getting good at are unreal and unimportant. They might laugh at him because he was no longer good at dealing with things in the cave. Finally, they might even act from their resentment and try to kill him. Still, down again he must go to help his fellow prisoners, and he must try to learn how to do that as well as he can.

Glaucon: If human life really is like life in the cave, then I can see why it would be dangerous for someone who had learned the truth about things to try to return to help those still there.

The Story of Fire
A Sufi Tale

Once upon a time, a man discovered how fire could be made. His name was Nour. He decided to travel from one people to another showing his discovery. He gave the secret to many tribes. Some people took advantage of what he taught them. Others drove him away, thinking he must be dangerous, without even waiting to see how valuable fire was. Finally a certain tribe became so frightened that they killed him, thinking he was an evil spirit.

Many years passed. In one tribe the knowledge about fire remained a secret known only to the priests. The priests were prosperous while the ordinary people froze. In a second tribe, the art of making fire was forgotten, but people continued to worship the tools of the fire-making. A third tribe worshipped a statue of Nour himself, because he had taught them about fire. In a fourth tribe, some kept the story alive, while others did not. Some people believed the story, others did not. A fifth tribe used fire in an everyday way—to keep warm and cook their food.

A wise man and his students were traveling through the land of these tribes. The students were amazed at all the ceremonies they discovered, and one of them said, "These ceremonies all have to do with the making of fire and nothing else. Let us teach these people the truth." The wise man said, "Very well. Let us start. By the end of this adventure, those of you who survive will know the real problems involved."

When they reached the first tribe, they were received in a friendly way. The priests invited them to attend their main religious ceremony, the making of fire. When it was over, the wise man said to his students, "Does anyone wish to speak?" One student said, "In the name of truth, I must speak to these people." "You do so at your own risk," said the master. The student stepped forward and said to the chiefs of the tribe, "I can also make fire, which you think is a miracle only the priests can perform. If I show you that you can do this too, will you admit that you have been wrong all these years?" But the priests broke in and said, "Take this man to prison." He was taken away and never seen again.

The wise man and his students then traveled to the lands of the second tribe, the one that worshipped the tools of fire-making. Again, another student offered to tell the truth to this tribe. He said, "I speak to you as reasonable people. You spend your time worshipping something instead of using it. You are not even worshipping the thing itself, fire, but the tools by which it is made. You stand in the way of progress. I know the truth about your ceremony." The people of this tribe were more reasonable. They said, "You are welcome as a stranger in our midst. But, because you are a stranger, you cannot understand our customs. You are mistaken. Perhaps you are even trying to take away our religion. We will not listen to you." The wise man and his students were forced to leave.

When they arrived in the land of the third tribe they found a statue of Nour, the firemaker, in front of every house. A third student spoke to the chiefs of this tribe. He said, "This statue is the statue of a man. It stands for a power which can be useful to everyone." "This may by so," said the worshippers of Nour, "but the discovery of the secret is only for the elite." The student then said, "You are refusing to face facts." The priests answered, "You are not a priest of Nour— you do not even speak our language well. Go away." The wise man and the students left.

They continued their journey and arrived on the land of the fourth tribe, the one which kept alive the story of the discovery of fire. A fourth student stepped forward and said, "This story of the making of fire is true, and I myself know how to do it." Confusion broke out in the tribe, and they split up into groups opposed to one another. Some said, "This story may be true, and if it is, we ourselves want to find out how to make fire." Many of those who wanted to find out about making fire were eager for advantage and not for human progress. Most ordinary people continued to believe the old stories about fire. They did not think fire was an everyday thing. The ones who thought these stories could show people how to make fire were often mentally unstable. They could not have made fire themselves, even if someone showed them how.

Other people in the tribe said, "We prefer our old stories. They give us something to believe together. What will happen to our community if we stop believing in them?" There were many other points of view also. The wise man and his students left. The wise man and his students had nothing to teach them.

They finally reached the lands of the fifth tribe where fire was in common use. These people were concerned about other things.

Thinking back over their trip, the wise man said to his students, "You have to learn how to teach, for men do not want to be taught. But first you have to teach people how to learn. Yet, even before that, you have to teach them that there is still something to be learned. People imagine that they are ready to learn, but they want to learn what they imagine must be learned, not what really must be learned. When you have learned this yourselves, then you can learn how to teach. Knowledge of something is different from knowledge of how to teach it to another."

The Autobiography
Benjamin Franklin

Early in my life, I conceived the bold and difficult project of arriving at moral perfection. I wished to live without committing any fault at any time. I wanted to conquer all the faults into which my desires, the customs of my society, and the urges of my friends might lead me. Since I knew, or thought I knew, what was right and wrong, I did not see why I might not always do the one and avoid the other. But I soon found that I had undertaken a task of more difficulty than I had imagined.

While my attention was taken up in guarding against one fault, I was often surprised by another. This is because I was in the habit of committing this fault, and my habit took advantage of my inattention to it. Also, my desires were too strong for my reason. I finally realized that although my mind was convinced that it was in my interest to act rightly, that belief was not enough to prevent me from slipping and continuing to commit faults. I had to break my old bad habits and acquire new good ones before I could depend on myself to act morally in a steady way. For this purpose, I invented the following method.

I made a list of the moral virtues I wanted to acquire. There were thirteen of them. To give an example of my method, I will talk about the one I call "Order." By "Order" I meant that I should arrange all aspects of my life so that I would always have enough time to do what I needed to do. My plan was to train myself to be in the habit of acting according to these virtues. I decided, therefore, not to practice them all together, but to practice them one at a time, and not to move on to the next until I had mastered the previous one.

To do this, I made a little notebook in which I devoted a page to each of the virtues. Everyday I made a note in the notebook whenever I failed to fulfill a particular one. I decided to give a week to practicing each virtue. Since there were thirteen of them, I had made up a thirteen-week course in moral virtue. I followed this plan for quite a long time. In the end, I found that I had made some progress in self-management, except that I couldn't correct my faults with respect to Order. Now that I am old, and my memory is bad, this fault bothers me even more.

I didn't arrive at the perfection at which I had aimed but fell far short of it. However, I became a better and happier man by the effort than I would have been if I hadn't tried at all. Thus, I was like a person who wanted to have the beautiful handwriting of experts. Even if his writing never gets as good as the experts, it does get better than it might have been otherwise.

Unit VI

Reflections on Peer Counseling

The Manual
Epictetus

Some things are in our power and control, while others aren't. It is in our power to decide what we think about things, and to decide which things we are going to pursue. It is also in our power to decide what we like and don't like. In a word, we control our own actions. Outside our power and control are all bodies in the world, including even our own bodies and our own property. Also, we have no control over our reputations and no control over whether people listen to us or not. Again, these are things that are not our own actions.

The things which are in our power are by nature free. Those which are not in our power are weak, slavish, and belong to others. Remember then, if you start thinking that slavish things are free, or that what belongs to others belongs to you, you will feel trapped. You will blame both gods and men. But if you suppose that what really belongs to you does belong to you, and that what really belongs to another does belong to another, you will be free. No one will ever force you. No one can ever stop you. You won't ever blame anyone for anything. You'll do nothing against your own will. You will have no enemies because no one will be able to hurt you.

If you decide to pursue such great things, you must also decide not to be attracted by money, property, reputation, and all the other things that are outside your control. You must give up some of them completely. The others you must postpone for the time being. If you want to be free, to have no enemies, to do nothing against your will, and at the same time to rule and control others and be rich, you will surely fail. You can become free and happy only if you gain power and control over yourself.

The Meno
Plato

Socrates: Come now, Meno, you must try to tell me what excellence as a whole is. Don't, as you have been doing, start telling me again about the excellence of a man as opposed to the excellence of a woman and how each of these differs from the excellence of a child. Tell me instead what excellence itself is.

Meno: It seems to me, Socrates, that excellence is what the poets say it is: to take pleasure in honorable things; to desire them; and to be able to get them.

Socrates: So you also say that he who desires honorable things desires good things?

Meno: Most certainly.

Socrates: Does this mean that some people desire good things and others bad things? Don't you think that all people desire good things?

Meno: No, I don't think so.

Socrates: You mean some people desire bad things?

Meno: Yes.

Socrates: Do they imagine that the bad things are good things, or do they recognize them to be bad and still want them?

Meno: In both ways, I think.

Socrates: Does it really seem to you, Meno, that someone can know that something is bad and still want it?

Meno: Certainly.

Socrates: Does this person want to possess it?

Meno: What else could he want?

Socrates: Does this person think the bad thing will benefit him, or does he know it will harm him?

Meno: Both things are sometimes true.

Socrates: In your opinion, do those who think the bad things will benefit them know that they are bad?

Meno: No, I don't think so.

Socrates: It is clear then that those who seem to desire bad things really don't. They really desire good things and make the mistake of thinking that certain bad things are in fact good.

Meno: That's how it seems to me.

Socrates: Do those, on the other hand, who know that bad things do harm, also know that these things will harm them if they do them?

Meno: They must know this.

Socrates: Does anyone want to be miserable?

Meno: I suppose not, Socrates.

Socrates: Therefore, Meno, no one really desires bad things. For what is being miserable but desiring bad things and getting them?

Meno: What you say seems true, Socrates. Nobody wants bad things.

Hiawatha Sees Himself
An Iroquois Tale

Deganawidah came to the house of a man who ate other humans. He climbed to the roof and lay down flat on his chest beside the hole where the smoke came out. There he waited until the cannibal came home carrying a human body, which he put into the kettle on the fire. The cannibal bent over the kettle and saw a face looking up at him. He was startled! It was Deganawidah's face; he was reflected in the water, but the man thought it was his own. In it was a wisdom and strength that he had never seen before nor dreamed that he possessed. The cannibal moved away from the kettle into the corner of the house. He sat down and began to think.

"This is a very wonderful thing," he said. "Nothing like this has ever happened before as long as I've lived in this house. I didn't know I was like that. A great man looked at me from out of that kettle. I'll look again and make sure that what I've seen is true." So he went over to the kettle again, and once more he saw the face of a great man looking up at him. "So it is true!" he said. "It's my own face in which I see wisdom and righteousness and strength. It certainly isn't the face of someone who eats other humans. It isn't like me to do that." He took the kettle outside and emptied it by the roots of a fallen tree. "Now I have changed my habits," he said. "I will no longer kill humans and eat their flesh. But that isn't enough. The mind is harder to change. I can't forget all the suffering I have caused. I have become very miserable."

The man felt his loneliness and said, "Perhaps someone will come here. Perhaps some stranger will come and tell me what I must do to make up for all the human suffering I have caused." When he returned to his house, he met Deganawidah, who had climbed down from the roof. They entered the house and sat down across the fire from each other. "Today I've seen a strange thing," said the man. "I saw a face looking at me out of the kettle: it was my own face, but it wasn't the face of the man who has been living here. It was the face of a great man. But I am not great, I am miserable."

"What happened today," said Deganawidah, "makes a very wonderful story. You have changed your life. A new mind has come to you, namely righteousness, health, and power. But you are now miserable because the new mind doesn't live at ease with your old memories. Your task will be to find a way to harmonize your new mind and your old memories."

A Philosophical Dictionary
Voltaire

Character comes from the Greek word for "impression or engraving." It is what nature has carved and engraved in us. Can we erase or change it? Great question. If I have a bent nose and two cat-like eyes, I can hide them behind a mask. Do I have more power or even as much over the character nature has given me?

A man born violent and hot-headed comes before King Francis I of France to complain about an injury. The appearance of the king, the respectful behavior of those near the king, and the size of the palace make a very powerful impression on this man. He lowers his eyes; his coarse voice becomes soft. He presents his petition humbly. One would think him as gentle as those courtiers who always go with the king. He is even confused while he is in this strange and unfamiliar place. But if the king can read faces, he will know everything he needs to know about this man. The king will easily discover in the lowered eyes a deep fire. By seeing the tightened muscles of this man's face and his lips pressed against each other, the king will realize that the man is not as gentle as he is now forced to appear. But the king doesn't notice these signs.

This man follows the king to war, and both are taken prisoner and thrown in jail. In prison, the king no longer makes the same kind of impression on the man. He begins to lose respect for the king. One day, while he is pulling off the king's boots and pulling them off poorly, the king, made bitter by misfortune, becomes angry. The man's violent temper comes back. He attacks the king, gets rid of him, and throws his boots out the window. As the Roman writer Horace said, "Drive out nature with a pitchfork; she'll always return."

Religion and ethics put a curb on nature's strength, but they cannot destroy it. The drunkard in a hospital, reduced to cider with his meals, will not get drunk any more. But he will always love wine.

Anger weakens character. Character is like a tree which, when it grows old, produces bad fruit but still of the same kind it used to produce. The tree becomes covered with knots and moss, becomes worm eaten, but it remains an oak or a pear tree. If we could change our character, if we could give ourselves a new one, we would be the master of nature. Can we give ourselves anything? Don't we receive everything? Try to stir up a lazy man with regular activity. Try to cool the boiling soul of someone who is reckless. Try to inspire the man who lacks taste or an ear for music and poetry. You would find it easier to give sight to a man born blind. We can improve, we can smooth down, we can hide what nature has placed in us. But we put nothing there ourselves.

A farmer was once told, "You have too many carp in this pond. They won't thrive and get fat. There are too many sheep in your fields. There isn't enough grass. They will grow lean." After he is told this, it just so happens that a larger fish eats half this farmer's carp, and wolves eat half his sheep. The rest of the carp in the pond and the sheep in the field thrive and fatten. What shall we say to this farmer? Should we applaud this man because of his good sense? This farmer is you. One of your desires or passions simply devours all the others, and you think you have triumphed over yourself. Don't we almost all resemble that ninety-year-old general who, when he ran into some young officers making a disturbance with some girls, said to them in great anger: "Gentlemen, is this the example I set you?"

Invisible Man
Ralph Ellison

I am an invisible man. No, I am not a spook like those who haunted Edgar Allan Poe, nor am I one of your Hollywood-movie ectoplasms. I am a man of substance, of flesh and bone, fiber and liquids—and I might even be said to possess a mind. I am invisible, understand, simply because people refuse to see me. Like the bodiless heads you see sometimes in circus sideshows, it is as though I have been surrounded by mirrors of hard, distorting glass. When they approach me they see only my surroundings, themselves, or figments of their imagination—indeed, everything and anything except me.

Nor is my invisibility exactly a matter of a bio-chemical accident to my epidermis. That invisibility to which I refer occurs because of a peculiar disposition of the eyes of those with whom I come in contact. A matter of the construction of their inner eyes, those eyes with which they look through their physical eyes upon reality. I am not complaining, nor am I protesting either. It is sometimes advantageous to be unseen, although it is most often rather wearing on the nerves. Then too, you're constantly being bumped against by those of poor vision. Or again, you often doubt if you really exist. You wonder whether you aren't simply a phantom in other people's minds. Say, a figure in a nightmare which the sleeper tries with all his strength to destroy. It's when you feel like this that, out of resentment, you begin to bump people back. And, let me confess, you feel that way most of the time. You ache with the need to convince yourself that you do exist in the real world, that you're a part of all the sounds and anguish, and you strike out with your fists, you curse and you swear to make them recognize you. And, alas, it's seldom successful.

One night I accidentally bumped into a man, and perhaps because of the near darkness, he saw me and called me an insulting name. I sprang at him, seized his coat lapels, and demanded that he apologize. He was a tall blond man, and as my face came close to his, he looked insolently out of his blue eyes and cursed me, his breath hot in my face as he struggled. I pulled his chin down sharp upon the crown of my head, butting him as I had seen the West

Indians do, and I felt his flesh tear and the blood gush out, and I yelled, "Apologize! Apologize!" But he continued to curse and struggle, and I butted him again and again until he went down heavily, on his knees, profusely bleeding. I kicked him repeatedly in a frenzy because he still uttered insults though his lips were frothy with blood. Oh yes, I kicked him! And in my outrage I got out my knife and prepared to slit his throat, right there beneath the lamplight in the deserted street, holding him in the collar with one hand and opening the knife with my teeth—when it occurred to me that the man had not seen me, actually; that he, as far as he knew, was in the midst of a walking nightmare! And I stopped the blade, slicing the air as I pushed him away, letting him fall back to the street. I stared at him hard as the lights of a car stabbed through the darkness. He lay there moaning on the asphalt; a man almost killed by a phantom. It unnerved me. I was both disgusted and ashamed. I was like a drunken man myself, wavering about on weakened legs. Then I was amused: Something in this man's thick head had sprung out and beaten him within an inch of his life. I began to laugh at this crazy discovery. Would he have awakened at the point of death? Would Death himself have freed him for wakeful living? But I didn't linger. I ran away into the dark, laughing so hard I feared I might rupture myself.

The next day I saw his picture in the *Daily News*, beneath a caption stating that he had been "mugged." Poor fool, poor blind fool, I thought with sincere compassion, mugged by an invisible man!

The Unhappiest Man
Soren Kierkegaard

An unhappy person is one who has his ideal and goal—that is, the essential part of his being—outside of himself. Such a person is always absent from himself. But it is clear that one can be absent from oneself in two ways. People are absent from themselves by living either entirely in the past or in the future.

There are some people who live in hope, and others who live in memory. Both these types are indeed, in a sense, unhappy people. They are unhappy to the extent that they live solely in the hope of something to come or in the memory of what was. This is because only a person who is present to himself is happy. However, in a strict sense, such a person is not entirely unhappy if he is at least present to himself as a part of his hope or as a part of his memory. So we must look further to get a more exact description of the truly unhappy person.

First, we shall consider the man of hope. When a man hopes, and he is not even present to himself as part of what he hopes for, then he is in a stricter sense unhappy. For such a person lives only for the future, and yet he does not believe himself to be a part of that future. Take an example. A man who hopes for eternal life has renounced the present. Such a person is, in a certain sense, unhappy, but not in the strict sense. For, at least, the eternal life he hopes for is for himself. He is therefore present to himself as a central part of his hope. But what if he even ceases being part of his hope. What if, time after time, he loses hope that eternal life is possible for him. He may hope for eternal life but believe that he will never gain it. Then he becomes more strictly unhappy, for his absence from himself covers not only the present but now also extends into the future. The case of the man who lives in memory is parallel. If he lives in the past and yet finds himself in those memories which absorb him, then he is not strictly unhappy. But if he is not part of his own memories, and so he is also absent from himself in the past, then we have yet another type of real unhappiness. Of the two cases, memory is the more important element of unhappiness. This is because the past has the remarkable characteristic that it is past. The future, on the other hand, is in a certain sense nearer the present than the past. The future is less absent than the past is.

In order for a man of hope to find himself as part of his hope, the future must have reality, or rather, it must have reality for him. Similarly, in order that the man who lives in memory may find himself in the past, the past must have had reality for him. But when a man hopes for a future which can have no reality for him, or a man remembers a past which has had no reality for him, then we have truly unhappy individuals.

It may seem that the first alternative is either impossible or sheer madness. However, this is not so. For though someone does not hope for what has no reality for him, he may hope for something which he knows cannot occur. And in the second case, a man who has nothing to remember may nonetheless continue to be a man of memory.

If someone buried himself in the Middle Ages or in his own childhood, and if these had genuine reality for him, he would now, in a strict sense, be an unhappy person. But imagine a man who had never had a real childhood. This age of life passed him by without attaining any real significance for him. Now he, perhaps by becoming a teacher, suddenly discovers the beauty of childhood. He now wishes to remember his own, but he had none. In such a person, we would have an excellent example of real unhappiness. He discovered and still wished to remember the importance of what he could no longer experience. Let us now imagine a man who lived without any appreciation of the real joys of life. On his deathbed his eyes suddenly opened to those things. Imagine further that he did not die (which would have really been better) but went on living though without living his life over again. Such a man would have to be seriously considered in our quest for the unhappiest man. The unhappiness involved in hope is never as painful as the unhappiness of memory. The man who hopes always has a more tolerable type of disappointment. So the unhappiest man will have to be sought from among the unhappy people who live in memory.

The Autobiography of Malcolm X
Malcolm X

I continued to think constantly about all that I had seen in Boston and about the way I had felt there. I know now that it was the sense of being a real part of a mass of my own kind for the first time.

The white people—my classmates, the Swerlins, the people at the restaurant where I worked—noticed the change. They said, "You're acting so strange. You don't seem like yourself, Malcolm. What's the matter?"

I kept close to the top of the class, though. The topmost scholastic standing, I remember, kept shifting between me, a girl named Audrey Slaugh, and a boy named Jimmy Cotton.

It went on that way, as I became increasingly restless and disturbed through the first semester. And then one day, just about when those of us who had passed were about to move up to 8-A, from which we would enter high school the next year, something happened which was to become the first major turning point of my life.

Somehow, I happened to be alone in the classroom with Mr. Ostrowski, my English teacher. He was a tall, rather reddish, white man, and he had a thick mustache. I had gotten some of my best marks under him, and he had always made me feel that he liked me. He was as I have mentioned, a natural-born "Advisor" about what you ought to read, to do, or to think—about any and everything. We used to make unkind jokes about him. Why was he teaching in Mason instead of somewhere else, getting for himself some of the "success in life" that he kept telling us how to get?

I know that he probably meant well in what he happened to advise me that day. I doubt that he meant any harm. It was just in his nature as an American white man. I was one of his top students, one of the school's top students—but all he could see for me was the kind of future "in your place" that almost all white people see for black people.

He told me, "Malcolm, you ought to be thinking about a career. Have you been giving it thought?"

The truth is, I hadn't. I never have figured out why I told him, "Well, yes, sir, I've been thinking I'd like to be a lawyer." Lansing certainly had no Negro lawyers—or doctors either—in those days, to hold up an image I might have aspired to. All I really knew for certain was that a lawyer didn't wash dishes, as I was doing.

Mr. Ostrowski looked surprised, I remember, and leaned back in his chair and clasped his hands behind his head. He kind of halfsmiled and said, "Malcolm, one of life's first needs is for us to be realistic about being a nigger. A lawyer—that's no realistic goal for a nigger. You need to think about something you can be. You're good with your hands—making things. Everybody admires your carpentry shop work. Why don't you plan on carpentry? People like you as a person—you'd get all kinds of work."

The more I thought afterwards about what he said, the more uneasy it made me. It just kept treading around in my mind.

What made it really begin to disturb me was Mr. Ostrowski's advice to others in my class—all of them white. Most of them had told him they were planning to become farmers, like their parents—to one day take over their family farms. But those who wanted to strike out on their own, to try something new, he had encouraged. Some, mostly girls, wanted to be teachers. A few wanted other professions, such as one boy who wanted to become a county agent; another, veterinarian; and one girl wanted to be a nurse. They all reported that Mr. Ostrowski had encouraged whatever they had wanted. Yet nearly none of them had earned marks equal to mine.

It was then that I began to change—inside.

I drew away from white people. I came to class, and I answered when called upon. It became a physical strain simply to sit in Mr. Ostrowski's class.

Where "nigger" had slipped off my back before, wherever I heard it now, I stopped and looked at whoever said it. And they looked surprised that I did.

I quit hearing so much "nigger" and "What's wrong?"—which was the way I wanted it. Nobody, including the teachers, could decide what had come over me. I knew I was being discussed.

In a few more weeks, it was that way, too, at the restaurant where I worked washing dishes, and at the Swerlins'.

One day soon after, Mrs. Swerlin called me into the living room, and there was that state man, Maynard Allen. I knew from their faces that something was about to happen. She told me that none of them could understand why—after I had done so well in school, and on my job, and living with them, and after everyone in Mason had come to like me—I had lately begun to make them all feel that I wasn't happy there anymore.

She said she felt there was no need for me to stay at the detention home any longer and that arrangements had been made for me to go and live with the Lyons family, who liked me so much.

She stood up and put out her hand, "I guess I've asked you a hundred times, Malcolm—do you want to tell me what's wrong?"

I shook her hand and said, "Nothing, Mrs. Swerlin." Then I went and got my things and came back down. At the living room door I saw her wiping her eyes. I felt very bad. I thanked her and went out in front to Mr. Allen, who took me over to the Lyons'.

Mr. and Mrs. Lyons and their children, during the two months I lived with them while finishing eighth grade, also tried to get me to tell them what was wrong. But somehow I couldn't tell them, either.

On Suspicion
Francis Bacon

Suspicions are to thoughts as bats are to birds. They always fly when the sun goes down. Suspicions should be repressed or at least kept in check, for they cloud the mind. They break up friendships and make it difficult to do business. Suspicions make kings into tyrants, husbands jealous, and wise men sad and indecisive. They are defects of the brain, not of the heart, for they affect even brave men. Brave people are not hurt by their suspicions, for they have the courage to examine them to see if they are true or false. Cowardly people, however, are hurt by suspicions, because they believe them too quickly. There is nothing that makes a man more suspicious than his own ignorance. Therefore, people should cure themselves of suspicions by trying to learn more, and not by brooding over them.

For what do you want out of people? Are the people we deal with everyday as good as saints? Isn't it true that people have their own interests and will be more concerned about themselves than about other people? The best way to handle suspicions is to assume that they are true, but to deal with them as if they were false.

For a man ought to use suspicions so that, if they are true, they will do him no harm. The suspicions to which a person comes on his own are harmless. They are like the buzzing of bees. Suspicions that have been put into a man's mind by the whisperings and stories of others are, like the stings of bees, harmful.

The best way for a person to find the road out of the forest of suspicions is to talk to the person he suspects. By this means he will find out more of the truth than he knew before. He will also make the other person more careful not to give him further grounds for suspicion. But this should not be done with dishonest people. For, if they once know that they are suspected, they will never again tell the truth.

The Doctrine of the Middle Way
Chung Yung

In all business dealings, success comes to those who prepare beforehand. Without this preparation, there will be failure. And when you are going to speak, you must decide beforehand what you are going to say. Then when the time comes, you won't slip up or stutter. And if before setting out on anything, you decide what you plan to do, you will not fall into confusion. Decide beforehand how you will act, and there will be no regrets.

Unless those who lead society have gained the confidence of those in the lower ranks, they will never get the support of the mass of the people. But there can be no confidence in leaders unless people who are friends can trust one another. And friends cannot trust one another unless they, in turn, do their duty to their own parents. And there is only one way which enables someone to do his duty. If a person is not true, he cannot do his duty to his parents. But there is only one way for a man to have a real and true self. He must understand what is good, for if he doesn't, he cannot be real and true in himself. The acts of a true man agree with his position and station in life. If he is a man of wealth, he acts as such. If he is poor, he acts accordingly. A man of wealth does not despise those who are poor. A poor man does not cling to those who are wealthy. Instead, he acts rightly and seeks no favors. If one acts according to one's station, one will feel no resentment towards others, nor will one be resented by others. One will have an easy mind and be prepared for whatever happens, unlike a man who is not true and keeps hoping for good luck. This is similar to target shooting. When a man who is true misses the target, he looks for the cause in himself.

Up from Slavery
Booker T. Washington

From the time when I could remember anything, I had been called simply "Booker." Before going to school it had never occurred to me that it was needful or appropriate to have an additional name. However, when I heard the school-roll called, I noticed that all of the children had at least two names, and some of them indulged in what seemed to me the extravagance of having three. I was confused because I knew that the teacher would demand of me at least two names, and I had only one. By the time the occasion came for declaring my name, an idea occurred to me which I thought would solve this situation.

When the teacher asked me what my full name was, I calmly told him, "Booker Washington," as if I had been called by that name all my life; and by that name I have since been known. Later in life I found that my mother had given me the name of "Booker Taliaferro" soon after I was born, but somehow that part of my name seemed to disappear, and for a long while was forgotten. But as soon as I found out about it, I revived it and made my full name "Booker Taliaferro Washington." I think there are not many men in our country who have had the privilege of naming themselves in the way that I have.

More than once I had tried to picture myself in the position of a boy or man with an honored and distinguished ancestry which I could trace back through a period of hundreds of years, and who had not only inherited a name, but also a fortune and a proud family home. And yet, I have sometimes had the feeling that if I had inherited these and had been a member of a more popular race, I should have been inclined to yield to the temptation of depending upon my ancestry and my color to do for me that which I should do for myself. Years ago I resolved that because I had no ancestry that anyone knew of, I would leave a record of which my children would be proud, and which might encourage them to still greater effort.

The influence of ancestry is important in helping any individual or race move forward, as long as not too much reliance is placed upon it. The very fact that a boy is conscious that, if he fails in life, he will disgrace the whole family record—extending back through many generations—is of tremendous value in helping him to resist temptations. The fact that the individual has behind him and surrounding him a proud family history and connections, serves as a stimulus to help him overcome obstacles when striving for success.

THIS PAGE MAY NOT BE REPRODUCED
OR DISPLAYED IN ANY FORM.

TOUCHSTONES® DISCUSSION PROJECT

Unit VII
Reflections on Serving the Aging

Anatomy of Melancholy
Robert Burton

1. In melancholy, one of the chief faculties of the mind, either reason or imagination, is corrupted. These powers of the mind are corrupted but not abolished and destroyed, which happens in madness. The ordinary companions of melancholy are fear and sadness, both of which are present without any apparent cause or occasion for them.

2. Those most subject to melancholy are people who are solitary and spend their time alone, who are great students, given much to contemplation and thought, and who lead a life of inactivity. Of the sexes, certainly both! However, men become melancholy more often; women, less often, but more violently and more deeply. Of the seasons, autumn is the most melancholy time. Of times of life, it occurs more frequently in those who are middle aged, between thirty or forty.

The Rhetoric
Aristotle

There are very great differences between young and old men. The young have strong desires, but these change very quickly. Their desires are very strong while they last but are quickly over. The young often get angry. This is because they love honor and can't stand being insulted. Therefore, they become furious when they imagine they have been treated unfairly. Yet, while they love honor, they love victory even more because the young are eager to feel superior to others. And they love both victory and honor more than money because they don't know what it's like to do without money. They look at the good side of everything because they haven't seen much wickedness. They are very trusting because they haven't been cheated much. All their mistakes come from overdoing everything. They both love and hate too much. This is because they think they know and are sure of everything. If they hurt others, it is because they mean to insult them rather than harm them. They are always ready to pity others because they think everyone is basically honest. They judge their neighbors by their own harmless natures and so can't believe that people deserve to be treated badly.

Old men are very different. They have often made mistakes and have been taken in many times. For them, life is bad business. The result of this is that they are sure about nothing and so always under-do everything. They "think" but never claim to "know." Because they are hesitant about everything, they add a "possibly" or a "perhaps" to whatever they say. Their experience makes them suspicious, and they think that everything is worse than it appears. They are not generous because money is one of the things they need, and they have seen how hard it is to get and how easy to lose. They lack confidence in the future partly because of the experience that most things go wrong and turn out worse than one expects. They live by memory rather than hope, for what is left to them of life is very little compared to what has passed. They are always talking about the past because they enjoy remembering it. Their anger is sudden but weak. They guide themselves by reason much more than by feeling, for reason is directed to what is useful; feeling to what is right. If they harm others it is because they want to injure them and not, as in the case of the young, to insult them. Both young and old men feel pity towards others. However, they feel pity for different reasons. Young men feel pity out of kindness. As was said, young men believe people are better than they really are and so don't deserve to be harmed. Old men, on the other hand, imagine that anything that happens to another might happen to them. And it is this possibility that stirs their pity.

Assignments for Reflecting on Service

A course with both service and class-work components should end with some type of written work which both documents and contains reflections on the students' experiences. Below are some sample questions which could be used for such a final piece of writing or as other assignments during the semester.

1. Describe the place where you are serving, including the sounds and smells.
2. What is the mission of the place where you serve? Do the people who work there do a good job? What would you do differently?
3. Describe the people you serve. Tell what a day is like for one of them. Can you generalize?
4. Across the country people serve our communities. What impact do you think this service has? Would you make more of an impact if you advocate for changes in laws?
5. Has doing service affected decisions you make or how you think about the needs of your community?
6. Describe someone you have gotten to know during service. What have you learned from this relationship?
7. Why do you think some people are in need? What could be done by them, by you, or by someone else to make their life better?
8. What was the best thing that happened in your service placement? What was the worst?
9. Now that you have served the community for a period of time, what are "Ten Tips" you have for future volunteers?
10. Why do you think Thomas Jefferson said, "A period of service is due from every individual"? What have you learned about democracy?